WHERE EAST MEETS WEST:

APPROPRIATING THE ISLAMIC ENCOUNTER FOR A SPIRITUAL-CULTURAL REVIVAL

To turn from the literature of Hindu-Buddhist-Taoist-Confucian Asia to that of Islam is, to a Westerner, like moving from a low hanging humid, all-embracing haze into an upper region of fresh, clean air. There is a realistic, explicitly expressed definitiveness about the Qur'an and its Islam which permits one of the West to breath more easily and to see things more clearly ... Islam gave to the West through its Arabian universities in Spain much of the source material and the enlightenment which made the West what it now is. Judaism, Christianity and Islam derive from common roots even though each adds its unique elements. There is the underlying solidarity of the Greco-Hebrew, Christian-Islamic world as well as the solidarity of Asia. Thus for a Westerner to move ... into Islam is ..., in a very real and fundamental sense to be coming home.

F. S. C. NORTHROP, *The Taming of the Nations* (1952)

A l'heure qu'il est, la condition essentielle pour que la civilisation européenne se répande, c'est la destruction de la chose sémitique par excellence, la destruction du pouvoir théocratique de l'islamisme ... Là est la guerre éternelle, la guerre qui ne cessera que quand le dernier fils d'Ismael sera mort de misère ou aura été relégué par la terreur au fond du désert. L'Islam est la plus complète négation de l'Europe; L'Islam est le fanatisme, comme l'Espagne du temps de Philippe II et l'Italie du temps de Pie V l'nt à peine connu; l'Islam est le dédain de la science, la suppression de la société civile; c'est l'épouvantable simplicité de l'esprit sémitique, rétrécissant le cerveau humain, le fermant à toute idée délicate, à tout sentiment fin, à toute recherche rationelle, pour le mettre en face d'une éternelle tautologie: Dieu est Dieu. L'avenir est donc à l'Europe et à l'Europe seule. L'Europe conquerra le monde et y répandra sa religion, qui est le droit, la liberté, le respect des hommes, cette croyance qu'il y a quelque chose de divin au sein de l'humanité.

ERNEST RENAN, *Inaugural Lecture, College de France,* (23 FEBRUARY 1862)

WHERE EAST MEETS WEST

APPROPRIATING THE ISLAMIC ENCOUNTER FOR A SPIRITUAL-CULTURAL REVIVAL

MONA ABUL-FADL

A REVISED EDITION

THE INTERNATIONAL INSTITUTE OF ISLAMIC THOUGHT
LONDON • WASHINGTON

NEW REVISED EDITION
1ST EDITION, 1992

The International Institute of Islamic Thought
P.O. BOX 669, HERNDON, VA 20172, USA
www.iiit.org

LONDON OFFICE
P.O. BOX 126, RICHMOND, SURREY TW9 2UD, UK
www.iiituk.com

ISBN 978-1-56564-354-3 PAPERBACK
ISBN 978-1-56564-353-6 HARDBACK

Typesetting and cover design by Sideek Ali
Printed in the United Kingdom by the MPG Books Group

CONTENTS

Note on this Revised Edition

IIIT has great pleasure in presenting this revised edition of Dr. Mona Abul-Fadl's *Where East Meets West: Appropriating the Islamic Encounter for a Spiritual-Cultural Revival.* The book was originally published under the title, *Where East Meets West: The West on the Agenda of the Islamic Revival.* Sadly, Dr. Abul-Fadl passed away in September 2008 before work on a revised edition could begin. Therefore, respecting the quality of her scholarship and in memory of her work no content or structural change has been made to the original edition, other than correction of typographical and other errors which had crept into the typesetting and design of the original.

PREFACE

IN presenting this book to the reading public, the International Institute of Islamic Thought places an important brick in the metatheoretical foundations of its Western Thought Project (WTP), for it was with the intent of encouraging an active and critical presence of the Muslim intellect that the broad outlines of the Western Thought Project were first conceived. Now, with the Publication of Dr. Mona Abul-Fadl's *Where East Meets West: The West on the Agenda of the Islamic Revival*, the Institute is confident that its Western Thought Project will bring about the discourse it envisions. This work represents a call by the Institute and its Western Thought Project to discriminating Muslim scholars the world over – a call to share in the development of an original, constructive, and intellectual Islamic stance as regards modern knowledge at both the conceptual and the methodological levels.

The author of this challenging work is a close and long-standing associate of the Institute. Abul-Fadl's work was first noticed by the former president of the Institute, *al-Shahīd* Dr. Isma^cil Raji al-Faruqi, and his wife, Dr. Lois Lamya' al-Faruqi. A meeting was arranged and, a few months before his assassination, al-Faruqi met with Abul-Fadl and came away from that meeting impressed by the scope of Abul-Fadl's reading, her knowledge of Western thought and tradition, and her ability to critize these both from Western and Islamic perspectives. Although al-Faruqi was anxious for Abul-Fadl to use her skills and knowledge for furthering the cause of the Institute's Western Thought Project, this did not materialize until after his assassination.

When she arrived at the Institute, Abul-Fadl took full responsibility for the Project, started processing materials which had been collected under al-Faruqi's supervision, and then began to cover new ground. After taking another look at the entire project in relation to the Institute's fundamental goal (the Islamization of knowledge), she drew up two charts offering two plans of action: one showed intellectual dealings with Western thought from an Islamic point of view, and the others showed academic cooperation and the preparation of synoptic textbooks in major academic disciplines. It soon became obvious, however, that preparing the envisioned systemic text books would require the continuous and combined efforts of a significant number of specialists – something which the Institute with its limited human and financial resources would find difficult to achieve within a reasonable period of time. This realization led the Institute to reconsider its priorities and strategies in addressing Western thought: it would now concentrate on developing a theoretical matrix of inquiry and providing a methodology for dealing with Western thought from an Islamic perspective. Both of these were done with the intent of understanding and evaluating Western thought in order to go beyond it after weighing it against the Islamic theory and sources of knowledge and the distinguishing traits of the Islamic imagination with its values vis-à-vis existence, humanity, and life.

Abul-Fadl decided to undertake the exploration of this vast field on her own. She went through hundreds of books and studies in order to immerse herself in the Western intellectual tradition, its roots, history, attitudes, and classifications. Over the next two years, Abul-Fadl recorded her ideas and observations in both English and Arabic. Then, gathering her data together, she submitted the first systematic report on the Western Thought Project, a work which documented her proposals and laid the groundwork in a manner that would be accessible to a cumulative, critical, or creative effort by others.

The report in itself is a serious study in the field, for it contains several constructive suggestions about how to deal with the logistics of undertaking such a monumental project. This report, together with its supplement of nearly six hundred pages, has not been published and at presents constitutes a reference for review and internal circulation. Indeed, Abul-Fadl might have been able to enrich the library of the Institute and of Islamic learning in general with several studies if only she had access to the same facilities as her Western colleagues. Often, the only thing a Western scholar needs to worry about is the idea itself, for the preparation, research, documentation, structured formulation, editing, correction, rewriting, and production of the final draft is commonly delegated to qualified research assistants and editors. If Abul-Fadl and many other Muslim thinkers could avail themselves of such facilities, the library of contemporary Islamic thought and culture would be a very rich one indeed.

In this volume, Abul-Fadl defines the Islamization of knowledge and elucidates the present state of thinking on this subject by explaining that one element of the Islamic religious imperative is to activate the Islamic worldview which, in turn, is contingent on the ideal of *tajaddud* (renovation). It is this ideal or commitment that the program of intellectual revival known as the Islamization of knowledge assumes.

The relevance of the Western Thought Project, Abul-Fadl further explains, is in reactivating the Muslim mind so that it can effectively interact within the contemporary epistemic chart, rather than merely introduce Muslims to the West or vice versa. What is at stake is a new type of encounter with the West in terms derived from the *tawḥīdī* episteme, so that a dynamic and equitable process of cultural interaction may be set into motion. The contemporary Islamic revival obliges Muslim thinkers to reconsider the world and their place in it, while the Islamization of knowledge (the revival's intellectual response) qualifies the nature of the Muslim's reconsidering the Other, particularly in the case of the West. Ultimately, by drawing on the sources of their rich spiritual heritage, Muslim scholars can effectively contribute to the resolution of many of the more acute social problems that threaten the course of an afflicted humanity.

Surely, too, this is a noble calling and and aspiration that must engage the hearts and minds of all those who share a stake in a better, nobler, and more humane world. It is a tribute to the WTP, as it is at present promoted by the Institute (IIIT) and as it is here ably outlined and formulated by the author, that it is all-embracing in its audience and concerns. True to the spirit of the faith and the message that inspired it, it is conceived in the conviction that the renewal of the Muslim intellect and the betterment of the condition of the Muslim Ummah are inseparably intellectual and spiritual enlightenment of all.

IIIT, 1412 AH/JUNE 1992

PROLOGUE

RECENTLY, an avant-garde Muslim critic stated that to have modern consciousness is to live in a world shaped by the Western mind. If in any doubt, one had only to reflect on how the contemporization of the world always entailed the Westernization of its mind.[1] This imposes a challenge to the modern Muslim who is called upon to reconcile his conscience as a Muslim with historical realities.

> The strategic goal of Islam's conscience and the grand problem of its thought concerns the realignment of the moral and the natural, including the historical worlds. The ultimate focus of Islamic discourse ... is the problem of world order, in which the West figures as one historical entity ... the Islamic tradition approaches the theme of universal order through a critical reflection on the human situation, both existentially within history and transcendentally within the self, from the Quranic thought categories of *ẓulm* and *ẓulm al-nafs*. The problem of relating the Islamic self to the world thus presents itself as a problem of world order which in itself forms a part of the more original and comprehensive theme of *ẓulm* in history and *ẓulm* in the soul. A critical theory of the self and the world that is derived from these two categories ... would go a long way towards ending the spell of spuriousness which victimizes Muslim thought at present.

At some point in shaping the Muslim discourse on conscience and history it will be necessary to reach out to others, particularly to the West itself, in order to evolve together the terms of a new global consciousness which is inclusive. In so doing the question which will inevitably arise is which West is to be expected to contribute to this encounter? Our critic predicates the answer to this question in the light of the commonality of interests which are likely to exist between the participants in the discourse. In this vein he suggests that:

> Not withstanding all the historical rivalry, the two faiths share a religious world view whose incontrovertible givens are God, man, history and revelation. As such there is considerable community of interest between Islam and Christianity which … (they) both lack vis- à-vis the modern West … (which embodies the "Faustian heresy") … Western atheistic humanism challenges the very *raison d'être of homo islamicus* (who is the *homo religiosus par excellence*). Why base a religion, culture, civilization and global community on faith in an unseen God, when man on his own can provide all the felicity, prosperity and power that has ever been achieved by any human society?

In this sense, then, reclaiming an Islamic consciousness means more than just repossessing the world as it now exists, as some modern critics might suggest. It entails reshaping the future of the global order along lines which are bound to be endorsed by the generic *mensch*, the *insān al-fiṭrah*, who also happens to be identical to homo religiosus. In this sense too, reclaiming an Islamic consciousness can mean the end of the modern predicament of an all-pervasive alienation – a theme which provides much of the animus for the soul-searching debate in the Western encounter with modernity.

The above glimpses of an intimate "dialogy" seen through the fragments of a discourse selected for a critical appreciation would suggest that, within Muslim intellectual circles, the debate on the West has already begun to take a turn unforeseen a few decades ago. The issue is no longer to defend the Islamic identity and heritage on the assumption that it qualifies Muslims for modernity, or that it is as good for Muslims as the standards set for the world by the West. Rather, the question is whether the standards of a modernity which may be seen to have imposed itself on the globe, West and non-West alike, are those most conducive to promoting the moral well-being, or even the physical survival, of the communities which constitute that world order. It is against this challenge that the Muslims are rediscovering the meaning and relevance of their Islamic heritage. At the same time as they recover their own identity and values in the light of that heritage, they strive to share it with others and to relate it to the world order of which all have become irrevocably bound. Yet history is real enough, and the balance and weight of a mixed historical experience between the West and the non-West in general, and that of the West and the Muslim world in particular, will have to be confronted if the future is not to be "ransomed" to the past.

It is with this understanding and vision, and with a sense of urgency drawn from reading the trend of the times, that the bid for renegotiating the terms of the global encounter is made here. It begins with a summons that is addressed to the intellectual community comprising both Muslims and non-Muslims. It urges on all concerned the need of reviewing their own attitudes and intellectual projects in the light of a fresh understanding of the context and needs in a global community/communion. The new understanding it proposes should draw on the principles and precepts enshrined in the authentic and verifiable sources of a divine guidance. The universality and timelessness of this guidance carry it beyond Muslims to non-Muslims and beyond the past into the future. This is an issue which will first have to be debated among Muslims for the sake of clarifying and articulating a coherent stance/stances on the score. The summons accordingly addresses Muslims in the first instance. But even as they debate amongst themselves, Muslims are part of a whole, and it is impossible not to take that whole into consideration even in the earlier phases of shaping the features of a new cultural response to the times. It is here too that renegotiating the terms of the encounter between the East and the West will have to be addressed in any such project of redefining cultural positions in a common world. On this account, the West figures on the agenda of a Muslim revival. On this account too, the repossession of their claims on history by the Muslims must be seen in terms of a new structure of empowerment, not of expropriation; it is a structure grounded in apportioning a share of dues to all who can responsibly stake their claims on a universal and noble trust.

The present volume is not in itself intended as an intellectual debate on the issue of the Muslim encounter with the West. Dimensions of this debate have already been taken up elsewhere and will continue to be the subject of future publications. Instead, the work at hand, as it stands, sheds light on a very practical project which has been on the agenda of the Islamic revival for some time and which has been addressed in different ways. Even when it has not been directly and exclusively broached, there is no doubt that the problem of the West figures significantly in any such agenda, as the historical attempts by Muslims to come to terms with the modern world in the past century so eloquently indicate.

One of the more original contemporary responses in this respect has come from the International Institute of Islamic Thought over the past decade. Its originality is due to the attempt to articulate and resolve this problem in a practical and comprehensive manner as part of a more general and fundamental need for restituting and reconstructing the modern Muslim mind. Already this terminology alerts us to the historicity of this process and draws attention to the current critical and reflexive turn among Muslims as they wrestle with the ravages of the postcolonial and, indeed, the precolonial condition. There is no doubt where the Muslim will take recourse in this process as he exercises his faculties of reasoned discrimination and enlightened understanding in locating his pristine sources and models. But this is not the place to expound on this theme, for our intention is merely to highlight the context and the spirit of the more immediate task. The problem of the encounter with the West then is being carried beyond the political and the economic arenas to an intellectual and an essentially cultural realm where it is conceived to properly belong. This is not to deny the importance of the other areas of encounter and exchange, but to give the latter activities and domains the depths which belong to the human civilizational venture.

To this end, the Institute published *The Islamization of Knowledge: General Principles and Workplan* in the early eighties and through it addressed the need for reconstituting the disciplines of modern inquiry in light of the Islamic precepts of knowledge. This was taken up as an element in a radical epistemic breakthrough in tackling the intellectual dimension. As work progressed it was more and more convincingly realized that the disciplines tendered in the modern academy were by-products and promulagators of a historical culture with its epistemologies and methodologies which were distinctive to an integral whole: the Western heritage. This could only mean that philosophy, history, and culture had to be tackled at a metadisciplinary level. A strategy was clearly needed for elucidating the nature and thrust of the knowledge chart of our times and for exploring the ways and means for its renegotiation. This is, no doubt, a demanding challenge which calls on the resources, the skills, and the imagination of all the community and which, indeed, invites an openness to others as well. The present slim volume responds to this need and articulates this realization. It is launched with the intention of sharing with all those concerned some of the initial conceptions as they are at present being developed within the Institute. The idea is to strive for their further enrichment and elaboration in the future by other contributions from an ever-expanding circle of interested, capable, and committed elements in the future. Let us briefly in closing touch on its background.

In the course of the spring of 1989, preparations were afoot at the Institute for a restricted round table on the Western Thought Project. *A Convocation* and a *Work Paper* were drafted to this end. When the meeting convened in the early summer, some background was given to participants on the nature of the project, its purpose, and its place in the overall Islamization of knowledge movement. What follows is a collection of these papers and the notes which were prepared for this session. It is hoped that publishing them in their essentially unpolished format might provide some food for thought to those who read them. More than what a "finished" product could achieve, the present material would hopefully prove to be a stimulus for taking up the threads and stringing them together in more original and thought-provoking directions.

MONA ABUL-FADL
Herndon, Virginia, USA, 1411 AH / 1990

CHAPTER I

A CONVOCATION: THE CULTURAL IMPERATIVE

The Cultural Imperative

THE fate of our civilization lies in the balance of culture, not power. Indeed, the terms of the culture of our times will determine the future of our politics and societies. Moreover, this simple truth applies equally to each constituent part of the global world, including the Muslim world.

Islam today continues to be, as much as it was in the past, at the hub and crossroads of contemporary civilization. The difference, from a historical perspective, lies in the West's control of the political setting, the primary factor in qualifying the terms of today's civilization, and in setting its pace and direction accordingly. These terms however are unsatisfactory, not simply on account of the inequities underlying Western power structures, but in view of the inadequacy of the cultural underpinnings which lend it its qualitative dimension. Any attempt therefore to influence the course of civilization must rely on the modes of interaction that occur between a dominant West and the emerging power centers all over the globe. In essence, these modes need to be seen as a function of culture and not merely as politics.

A digression here may place this relationship in due context. It goes without saying, or so it would appear, that the prospect of rival power centers conjures the image of a scramble for substituting one hegemony for another. But this should remain at the level of an assumption open to historical refutability. Admittedly too, the emergent power centers are bound to constitute a threat to the current dominance of the West through their challenging its supremacy. The implications of this challenge, however paradoxical it may appear, need not necessarily imply a loss for the West; it can indeed mean, through its consequences for the global system, a net gain for all the parties concerned. Obviously, however, this is not a foregone conclusion.

To the extent that the emergent power centers develop in the context of the prevailing power economy, rooted as it is in the domination/subjugation model, the outcome can only be conceived in terms of a zero-sum game. To the extent, however, that the emergence of these power centers brings with it the possibility of an alternative to the conflict model, the challenge must be conceived in terms of its implications for a new paradigm of world order that transcends the constituent identities of those who are the parties to this order.

The possibility of this alternative is contingent on the cultural factor, not the political. The significance of the Muslim world as an emergent power center lies in its claim to a cultural identity and heritage that qualify it for a paradigmatic contribution of this nature. In order for it to assume its role, however, it is essential that it revive its culture, recover its *tawḥīdī* ontology, and rediscover and activate its episteme, all of which call for a measure of cultural autonomy. Given the nature of the world system and the historical realities of the Muslim Ummah, the extent to which this may take place is severely restricted. In considering the need for such autonomy, the limitations imposed by pervasive cultural penetration and hegemony will have to be addressed. This may be an onerous task, but it invokes its own ardour; one that is only augmented by necessity.

To assure the premises for a cultural revival, it will be necessary to give priority to consolidating a measure of cultural autonomy. This calls for redressing the anomalies of the prevailing cultural imbalance between the Muslim world and the West. The difficulty lies in defining boundaries in a context where the very rationale of autonomy becomes problematic. Reviewing the West becomes in part a process of reviewing the self in its contemporaniety. Having become an endemic feature of the cultural setting in the Muslim world itself, the culture of the West can neither be neglected nor ignored. However, it is the way in which this pervasive intrusion is approached which constitutes the difference and the challenge. Hitherto Muslims have been at the receiving end, and the prevailing logic of encounter has oscillated between a dialectics of imposition and a dialectics of seduction. In the tidal revival in the Muslim soul, the recovery of the consciousness of self and identity is currently accompanied by an appreciation in self-confidence and a revalorization of the Muslim identity. This has reflected positively on various attitudes, include those relating to the enduring encounter with the West.

The novelty here lies in the initiative taken by Muslims to evolve a serious and credible reading of the West. They realize that they will first need to understand the West in its own terms before they can evolve an objective and critical reading of their own. On the other hand, they equally realize that unless they can develop a viable and credible Islamic platform for their intellectual venture, their critical and discriminating aptitudes will be severely impaired and their version of the account of the West will be of dubious value. Furthermore, it may be pointed out that, for Muslims, such a reading of the West cannot be an end in itself; it is valued more for its potential contribution to redressing the intellectual equilibrium of an entire culture that finds itself threatened. The core of that threatened culture lies in the Muslim hemisphere, but its range and reverberations embrace the globe.

The value of a revival which takes its measure from an Islamic core lies in an implicit model of world order more congenial to the times and more compatible with the needs of the future. It is a model that bears the imprints of a global universality that stops short of abrogating the centers of autonomy. The proverbial capacity for accommodating diversity within the parameters of unity has, in the past, constituted the hallmark of the historical civilization of Islam. There is no reason why this should not be so in the future. In this sense, an Islamic reading of the West can contribute to the sanctification of the culture of the West, not to its subversion. Meanwhile, it will contribute to redressing the global balance of culture to the advantage of other less advantaged centers as well. In this way, it would also be contributing to the safeguarding of all parties from their own excesses. At the bottom line, an Islamic reading of the West will signify the rebirth of an authentic tradition of learning and knowledge that has for long been unjustifiably submerged. Through redressing the anomalies of a civilizational perversity, the excesses of the prevailing paradigm may be alleviated.

The International Institute of Islamic Thought, as one of the many robust young institutions which the first decade of the fifteenth century *hijrī* has spawned, has consecrated itself to the cultural imperative. Lying within the range of the Institute's priorities, the Western Thought Project is significantly conceived as part of a comprehensive and systematic workplan which is essentially flexible. It is open to periodic revision and "upgrading" in the light of a growing experience in the field and its anticipated contribution to a concomitant conceptual sophistication. The essentials of the plan, however, remain. These are predicated on a close-knit set of principles that are logically integrated and bound up together through an underlying revivalist rationale. The following is a recapitulation of these principles as they are briefly expounded against this rationale:

(1) The *Workplan* begins with a fresh reading of the Qur'an and the Sunnah on the understanding that they continue to constitute now, as much as in the past, the enduring foundations for any viable Islamic civilization. These are the wellsprings and immutable sources of an Islamic culture and knowledge, and any genuine intellectual essor in the Ummah is contingent on the efficacy of this fresh reading in the modern context.

(2) This is corroborated by a critical and objective reassessment of the Muslim cultural and intellectual heritage of the past to sift out the wheat from the chaff. The nature of the modern intellectual essor calls for a reflexive and reflective interaction with the thought processes and products of past generations as they responded to the challenges of their times in the context of the Islamic moorings of their civilization. The counterpart to this reflexive and reflective interaction may be found in the Muslim assessment of the modern heritage projected by the West.

(3) It acknowledges the necessity of a similar critical and objective reassessment of the Western mind, its processes, and its cultural and intellectual artifacts. The objective is to develop the insight necessary for discerning its strengths and weaknesses, the negative and the positive aspects that are to be found in another distinct legacy, and to identify its sustaining dynamic and mechanisms of production, transmission, and reproduction, or perpetuation.

(4) The objective is to develop a valid methodology that will enable the reconstruction of the modern Muslim mind along lines that will ensure the recovery of its originality and creative potential. Given the premises of the venture, the lessons learnt in the course of critical cultural exposure and in the reflexive dynamic of intra- and cross-cultural interaction, a distinct Islamic vision will crystallize and this, in turn, will generate a fresh civilizational impulse in our own time.

In assuming a responsibility on this scale, the Institute is under no illusion as to the enormity of the task and the limitations of the available resources. It is, nevertheless, intent on contributing, to the best of its ability, its share to the realization of an impending historical ideal – if only to constitute itself as a model to the Ummah and to provide the stimulus that others might follow. To this end, it has taken it upon itself not only to articulate the ideal and thus to actively promote it Ummah-wide, but, furthermore, to spare no effort in mobilizing the talents and the competences needed to ensure the most effective mode of implementation. Each phase of the *Workplan*, each facet, and each level of its implementation calls for a variety of such competences. In the final analysis, the substantiality of the achievement is contingent on the complementariness of these efforts. The Institute has been established in order to tap new potential, to encourage and preside over an expanding pool of resources, and to see that an effective coordination is sustained without losing sight of the purposeful orientation of the whole enterprise. This too is the operational context in which the conception and the implementation of the Western Thought Project takes place.[1]

Beyond any immediate plans, there is a need to bring the Western Thought Project into clear focus and to overcome any inertia on this front of the workplan. The idea of interlocking round tables to debate on the Western Thought Project, or aspects of it, is expected to mark an important landmark in promoting a greater consensus of opinion among Muslim scholars and intellectuals on an issue that is critical to the long-term prospects of an Islamic cultural revival. In the final analysis, success will be contingent on the ability to systematically set out the terms of the modern encounter with the West along lines more conducive to a genuine parity of cultures.

CHAPTER II

CHARTING A COURSE: BEYOND THE FAUSTIAN DELUSION

Beyond the Faustian Delusion

THE Western Thought Project is part of an extensive program to Islamize knowledge. This program calls on modern scholars to review the products and processes of modern culture, including their modes of thought and their fields of scholarship, from a perspective which looks at the sources and standards of the Islamic episteme. In view of the secular origins of modernity, the force of this appeal lies in its challenge to the exclusiveness and the validity of the prevailing episteme. In essence, Islamization contests the reductionism of this episteme and questions its validity. In making the case for an alternative model, it is opening new possibilities for a discourse which will admit new participants who may share elements of its particular Islamic perspective on knowledge. This would include the scholarship cultivated in the living traditions of the culture areas of the globe, as well as that coming from the biblical tradition in the West. However the Islamic episteme brings with it, in addition to its transcendental sources, a historical model of learning with a wide-ranging scope of *mundane* interests. In this sense there may be grounds for convergence with certain aspects of modernity, without conceding its foundations and ordering framework.

How the Western Episteme Came to Dominate

The dominant epistemological mode today crystallized during the epoch of the European Enlightenment which reached its apogee in the course of the eighteenth century. Then, in the following century, the latent historical trends bred in the early modern period – circa sixteenth century and after – led to the inflation of the power of Europe and culminated in its domination of the globe by the turn of the twentieth century. Its ideological bias notwithstanding, Immanuel Wallerstein's model of the world economy distinguishing the center from the periphery, with a Western European culture zone occupying the former and a loose amalgam of Afro-Asian and Latin overlapping culture zones constituting the latter, provides a reasonable classification of this development.[1] In this way, the diffusion of the Enlightenment model followed in the tracks of the advancing hegemony of the West to challenge and dominate in its turn. With the balance of power in favor of the rising West, there was little chance for a parity of exchange in this modern encounter of cultures. Where the regional culture survived, despite the onslaught of the intrusive power-backed culture into their field, they would continue to survive in a submerged state.

The Globalization of the West

For all intents and purposes then, the triumphant Western culture would henceforth assume the character of a global culture exerting its influence for good and evil on every other people. In practical terms, this meant that the standards of acculturation to the times were those set by the West, and that the global aspiration for modernity, to which the peoples of the Third World turned in their national development programs, really constituted a more euphemistic expression for a blatant Westernization. From there it was easy to confound the paradigms of modern and Western and to project the universality of the Western heritage.

In the meantime, the twentieth century in the Western world saw significant flux in the cultural climate nearer home. Although the forebodings were there earlier on, by the closing decades the exuberant optimism which had marked the onset of the century had to all intents and purposes become extinguished. There was an impoverishment in philosophy, the cornerstone of the Western intellectual tradition, and theology, periodically resuscitated from recurrent bouts of exhaustion, could hardly shoulder the burdens of a new transitional epoch unfolding in the guise of a "postmodernity." Confusion and skepticism became pervasive. Today, the metatheoretical debates in the social sciences and the humanities reflect and reinforce this general desultory mood.

The Opening Out of the West

If there is one advantage to be sought in this condition, it is perhaps to be found in a new disposition of openness in the Western mind together with, or in spite of, an inclination to a growing measure of introspection. The West is opening up to its past, seeking to "remember" in ways it has not done for nearly two centuries. It is more significantly searching out neglected elements of its past in ways it has not done since its earlier renaissance. Where the Enlightenment had sealed certain gates to the modern mind, the contemporary phase of high modernity seems to be reopening them. An example may be sought in the revival of the debate on the limits of human rationality and a renewed interest in the possible relevance/meaning of revelation.[2] On the other hand, the West is seeking its past today in a historically transformed context where history is no longer a closed stage, and where it is no longer the only hero in the play. In other words, there is today a noticeable disposition on the part of the modern/postmodern West to turn to other cultures and traditions in an anticipation that they too might have something to offer. This is presumably done in the spirit that there is something there to be learned. There is still, however, a long way to go before this quest is approached in a spirit where curiosity is tempered more by humility than pride. The time has not yet come for the Western scholar to willingly squat at the feet of an Indian guru.

More particularly, in the case of Islam, the West is afforded a ready cultural arena, which in more ways than one is nearer to the West than any other oriental tradition. F.S.C. Northrop's genuinely enlightened remark, cited as an epigram to the present volume, comes to mind.[3] It constitutes a perspicuous and honest confession, although admittedly it may not be the most representative of its kind. The opposing reflection by the free-thinking French philosopher, Ernest Renan (1823-1892), who supposedly projected the historical Enlightenment in all his works, including his secular inquiry into the life of Jesus (*La vie de Jésus*), affords a dramatic illustration of the more typical attitude in this regard.[4]

Fortunately, this brand of vitriol is losing its edge: and so it must, of necessity, if not of prudence. Yet the attitude of the West continues to be hedged in by a persistent ambiguity. The legacy of the historical encounter, compounded by the politics of contemporary times, makes the opening up to the Islamic heritage and to its heirs far more problematic. The initiative here will have to be taken by Muslims, although if the interaction is to gain momentum it will have to be reciprocated by responsiveness from the West. The real question though is this: Are Muslims prepared and qualified for this kind of initiative?

The new *daᶜwah*, or the summons to "Islamize" knowledge is a move in this direction.[5] It renounces claims to power in favor of a bid for truth and it gives priority to politics of culture and cultural reconstruction rather than to a culture of politics and power-mongering. Knowledge may be a means to power, but it is also an access to virtue and wisdom, and the Islamic perspective on knowledge has much to offer in a direction that reconciles antagonisms and dissolves artificial dualisms. In other words, this Islamization of knowledge brings into circulation a currency that is much needed by the times. In its appeal to knowledge, it appeals to common symbols which, once understood, cannot fail but to command a widening and deepening allegiance of a variety of scholars from all walks and hues. However, the immediate challenges to the Islamization of knowledge may not lie in the West, where it is out to contest the foundations of its still dominant paradigms, but in quarters nearer home.

Thus far, we have made the case for Islamization largely in the context of a Western perspective. We have suggested that the West is currently going through a process of rethinking its own heritage and that it is doing so in a relative openness to its own past as well as to the cultural experience of others. The catalyst to this critical re-examination is the deadlock which has ensued from the West's becoming hostage to a reductionist paradigm of knowledge and being that has found its way to the Western, and now a pseudoglobal, mind in the gospels of the Enlightenment and Modernity. We have also suggested that in the attempt to transcend the present predicament, Islam as culture, episteme, and heritage has much to offer the West and the modern world, to the extent that the latter has become Westernized or to the extent that the West has arrogated to itself the category of universality. The anomaly, however, lay in the obstruction caused by an essentially subjective dimension which was likely to impede access to an available Islamic model.

Auspicious Anticipations

The implication so far is that a free and open interchange between the West and Islam could not be left to the West to initiate, and that on the contrary, the Muslims would have to pave the way to this end. Indeed, we might go so far to suggest that once the historical and subjective barriers have been effectively addressed, then the principles animating the plea for the Islamization of knowledge are as likely to find fertile soil in the West as they are within the historical Islamic heartland. Nonetheless, a shift of perspectives is needed to allow us to examine the Islamization of knowledge and the Western Thought Project within the Muslim context.

Charting the Muslim Setting: Cultural Cleavages/Blockages

In the Muslim heartland, the triumph of the Enlightenment model still seems to carry the day and, ironically, it would seem to inspire greater loyalty there among some of its devotees than it would among its own veterans in the West. However, this observation must be qualified by the realization that the cultural milieu here is severely strained, for the Western model, however pervasive, remains subject to all the constrictions which attend an intrusive culture. Meanwhile, the home culture, which continues to be thoroughly Islamic, has shown its resilience in its persistent appeal not only to the masses, but also carries it to a growing proportion of the modern educated sectors of the public. This resilience, however, bespeaks a latent or a potential, rather than an effective vitality. The latter is contingent on the state of its scholarship, and this, for various reasons, has been hamstrung and hemmed in by debilities of its own which antedate the colonial interlude, although the latter no doubt precipitated the corrosion.

Cultural Immobility

The general setting in the Muslim heartland is immobilized by a complicity of factors. The discontinuities in the intellectual circles among the pockets of the thoroughly, moderately, and ambiguously Westernized on the one hand, and the uncompromising adherents to the Islamic heritage on the other creates a permanent fissure at a critical node in the prevailing culture. Rarely, however, is the breach complete. Indeed, a truer picture would be of a murky and blurred pool subject to conflicting currents diluting and diffracting the input from the different sources. Nowhere is this more conspicuous than in the educational establishment, itself so central to the processes of cultural production, transmission, and reproduction.

Afflictions of the Traditionists

For various reasons, rational and otherwise, Islamist circles are immobilized by their own divisions, reluctances, and rigidities in such a way that any renovationist appeals are likely to be resisted as much out of an instinctive and cautious reserve as out of any genuine religious or academic factor. There may be a vague awareness among Muslims in this group that they do indeed preside over the seeds of a genuine intellectual and cultural renewal, but then they are too submerged in their own inadequacies to be able to articulate this awareness. Those who might be in a position to do so are themselves hopelessly out of touch with their culture, and their plight is doubly compounded by a false sense of confidence deriving from an illusion that they are living their age. In contrast to the traditionists who hark back to a cultural heritage they are unable to animate, there are the modernists who have made some bold leaps across space and time. Their greatest merit, though, lies more in their conspicuity than in their perspicuity.

Self-Banished Exiles

The modernists or the Westernizers in the Muslim cultural spectrum are self-banished exiles to a no-man's zone where they are stranded in the twilight of a cultural "metaxy" – a cultural in-between. Their position is more pathetic than heroic, since they are doomed to fighting a doubly losing battle. They claim to be out to transform a culture and breathe new life into it, when in fact they little realize how presumptious is their claim. A resilient culture has its own mechanisms and dynamics which defy an exogenous approach to tamper with it. In presuming to act on a culture, they lay untenable claims to a capacity to influence and a power to act which they do not in fact sustain. For one thing, in renouncing their historical culture they are seen to have opted for foreign loyalties – and as far as the core of Muslim community goes, no amount of rationalization can conceal the fact that they have abdicated a trust and forfeited their claims to be the representatives of a culture.

The affective element is compounded by a cognitive one, as these modernizing/Westernizing elements have also succeeded in marginalizing themselves from their own culture by depriving themselves of its medium of communication. Lost to their adopted language and its values and symbols, they further fade into an illusory cultural horizon which they seek to perpetually create and recreate by a simulated vitality. Indulging in their brand of sterilities, they remain peripheral to the culture they claim to transcend but which they have in effect betrayed. Wherever their influence surfaces, they proclaim it as testimony to their virtuosity and enlightenment. In fact, this serves as a poignant reminder of the pervasiveness of the cult of power in the contemporary Muslim world, where culture has become an industry contingent on organizational and manipulative skills and carries little affinity for the virtues of knowledge and learning. In making this statement, we have in mind the dominance of Westernized coteries in the ruling elites throughout the Establishment, including the all-important media sector, which is the case in most Muslim countries today.

Changing Contexts

However, by definition the cultural situation is a fluid one, and times are changing. In some circles, Islamic sensibilities are becoming more alive and, in others, a new sensibility has been provoked by the awareness of the pervasiveness of an enduring Islamic reality. Modernists are no longer as prone to dismiss the relevance of the Islamic cultural heritage in their attempt to address their times. Islamists are no longer immune to the disaffections of the age and are increasingly awakening to the futility of their own defensiveness and to the need for overcoming their self-imposed closure in their attitudes to their cherished heritage as well as to an alien world. It is these stirrings in the wind that blows over the Muslim landscape that have been invariably expressed in different forms and arenas and which have been dubbed the Islamic revival. They are in reality the signs and symptoms of a recovery of identity and consciousness and the rebirth of a resolve to have a historical presence.

In steadily coming to terms with the self in the Muslim heartland, the modernists may not have changed their goals in opting for modernity, but they have at least evinced a flexibility and a willingness to review their means as well as in formulating their goals. Islamists too are now more disposed than ever to reflect more critically upon their history, since the coming of the era that signalled the rupture of their Islamic history, and they are more inclined to examine the consequences of the great intrusion represented by the colonial interlude. Here and there, there is a dawning awareness that what is amiss in the present must have its roots in the past, and that the will to break into the future is contingent on an honest and critical reexamination of a number of contingencies and categories including the self, the other, and the historical situation that embraces and conditions the cultural leavening.

Without realizing it, the gaps and schisms between the different circles are narrowing, as traditionalists and modernists are coming to stand on converging grounds: simply as Muslims striving to reconcile the self to the age without denying the one or renouncing the other. In seeking to preserve and safeguard the tradition which is the foundation of their identity and the cornerstone of their history in the future, it is increasingly realized that innovation and renovation are the requisites to the goal. This inevitably calls for reviewing the relationship of the traditional, i.e., it calls for a new, vibrant, and relevant reading of the Islamic heritage. Conversely, the unmistakable salience, relevance, and dynamic of the latter has forced itself on the attention of the cultural defectors of a more recent past, and as they too find a place in their agenda to review it in the light of their priorities, they may also come to realize that modernity itself is a negotiable destination. The crux of the matter may indeed lie in a new reading of modernity, and it will perhaps be on this platform that the terms of a new encounter between Muslims and the West will unfold.

The Nature of a Summons

It was in this general setting that the Islamization of knowledge was launched as a catalyst to a more critical and reflective mood, invigorating the process of self-examination and giving it direction. The Islamization of knowledge is explicitly targeted at examining, exposing, and transposing the characteristic modes of thought and learning current among Muslims. Moreover, it seeks to raise an awareness of the nature and the process of cultural formation, reformation, deformation, and mutation in the Ummah with a view to generating a genuine renovationist momentum in its ranks. The idea is to articulate and develop an Islamic episteme that will inspire the standards and criteria which may be used to institute and rationalize alternative thought modes and cultural output.

Scope of Address

While the Islamization of knowledge is primarily addressed to Muslims as a away out of their cultural and civilizational malaise, its message is by no means exclusive. Two factors preempt any such exclusiveness. The one inheres in the intrinsic universalistic calling of the Islamic standards which are being invoked as the measure for cultural sanification. The other evokes the inherent characteristics of the situational contingency, as was shown above, a matter which equally obviates any notion of complete cultural autonomy in a system of global hegemony. In this context, rethinking the dominant culture calls for a fresh reading of the West and its legacy. Given its premises and its objectives, this reading stresses objectivity and originality as much as relevance and utility. In this way, an Islamic reading of the modern West becomes an integral part of any program aimed at rectifying the cultural scales in the Muslim world. By the same token, this reading is likely to be as relevant to the West itself in its own soul-searching. These are the yields of mutuality in an age of global interdependence.

Appropriating Global Interdependence to Promoting Islamic Goals

By absorbing the Muslim ecosphere within the sphere of its own hegemony, the West has made it impossible for Muslims in the modern world to contemplate their cultural survival as a distinct civilizational entity, or their renewal as such, without also addressing their predicament from within the global framework. The great transmutation referred to by Marshall G. S. Hodgson has indeed made some version of Western culture endemic to the local setting of practically every urban center in the world today, including the Muslim centers.[6] This has its positive implications to the extent that the Muslim reading of their particular text must produce a corresponding reading of the global text as well. Just as addressing the Western heritage becomes an imperative in restituting the cultural chart in the Muslim world, it might also be conceded that the efforts produced in the venture are likely to affect a restitution at the global level as well.

The Idea of a Profitable Exchange: A Tijāratan Rābiḥah[7]

Conversely, this transmutation has come, in turn, to exact its retribution in kind as the circulation of influence can no longer be confined to its original concerted and authoritarian version. The West can no longer monopolize the reading of its own culture any more than it can claim such prerogatives for the culture of the other. As long as it maintains its capacity to learn from its own insights as well as those of others, it can only reap the benefits of the breakdown of an erstwhile monopoly. The rules apply to all the players. To the extent that Muslims are willing and able to produce their version of the global text, they will be contributing to transforming a dominant, one-track model into a diffusion model where ideas, unlike commodities and power-interests, will create their own trajectories. It is in this sense that the above assumption about the balance of modern civilization resting on culture rather than power should be understood. Ultimately, the reading of the one and the other are not exclusive. Once a perspective coming from the Islamic episteme finds its way into the global cultural horizon, it will then be possible to conceive of an alternative mode of thinking which goes beyond the either/or matrix to one where the options included the "both and more" variant. But this can only crystallize as the Western Thought Project advances and as the Islamization of knowledge platform is consolidated.

We may sum up the point of what we dubbed at the outset as the passing of the Faustian delusion in a key statement. Coming as it does at this juncture in time, and conceived in the cultural context of Islamization, the Western Thought Project acquires a particular significance. The end of modernity in the West, and the dawning self-consciousness beyond, beckons the emergence of a new discourse which can overcome the prevailing sense of moral depravity and intellectual aridity which threatens to engulf all in an age where boundaries fuse. In order that it might persuade and pervade, this discourse will also have to infuse the kind of vitality and direction which are currently lacking. For various reasons which have been mentioned elsewhere, the Western Thought Project in its Islamizing habitat is assumed to meet with the measure of this discourse. Whether it is seen from a strictly Muslim perspective or from a more general one, the relevance of this project can hardly be overemphasized. Nor can its urgency be overlooked.

CHAPTER III

PRIMARY PERSPECTIVES: THE ISLAMIZING CONTEXT

The Islamizing Context

THE past decade has witnessed the stirrings of the Islamic intellectual revival. A renewed interest in self, other, and history has accompanied the anticipations and aspirations born of the revival. Islamization of knowledge as a concept has become the shorthand for this intellectual orientation, and the Western Thought Project needs to be seen as an integral part of a more comprehensive program to consolidate the revival. This Project signifies an interest by Muslims in the West, and it is in this sense that the term "encounter" has been used in drafting some preliminary working papers on the subject.[1] It also signifies a renewed and intensified interest by Muslims in their own fate as it has been overshadowed by the West in the context of a disadvantaged moment in their historical encounter.

Two years ago efforts were made to follow up on the Project as it was initially conceived in the *Islamization of Knowledge: General Principles and Workplan*.[2] The following are excerpts – direct and paraphrased – taken from the preface of a report evaluating and describing this project which was submitted by the author to the policy council at the International Institute of Islamic Thought. These excerpts give some insight into the conception of the Project, its nature and its objectives, as well as into the spirit in which it is being pursued. They also place this conception within the framework of a more general understanding of culture and cultural change. Within the immediate context, however, the Project is conceived in terms of an Islamizing perspective, and this explains the acronym *RECTOCC*, for Re-Evaluating the Cultural Topography of the Occident. Its general tone and approach is simple but, hopefully, not simplistic. Clearly, the purpose at hand is not to investigate an area, but to delineate it and to point in a direction which could eventually pave the way for evolving a cultural hermeneutic open to more concerted, systematic, and innovative inquiry in the future and involving a widening circle of competences. Ultimately, the Project remains the responsibility and the charge of the entire Ummah.

A Synoptic Overview[3]

At the threshold of the revival, Muslims are taking a fresh look at their own heritage and at that of the contemporary world in which they live. A new consciousness is taking shape, and part of it is the realization that culture is a deliberate and planned growth that must be nurtured and tended if it is to express the willed identity and the aspirations of a people. In the absence of this realization, there will be fragments and pockets in an amorphous whole constituting inroads into a barren cultural field beyond which hovers the void. By definition, culture must be cultivated, and unlike things, it cannot be imported. In order for Muslims to cultivate an authentic culture, they need to develop a critical awareness of their own heritage as well as that of others, primarily of the dominant heritage which is of the West. Only then can they resume an effective and creative presence on the cultural and epistemic horizons of a global civilization. Only then too can they recover their lode-star role in history as a credible force for justice and right among nations: a witness unto humankind.

It was such ideas that prompted the advocates of the Islamization of knowledge to adopt a systematic and a practically oriented approach to the needs of planning the intellectual essor of the ummah. Opening a new window on the West with a view to critical appreciation and reflection on that heritage as it is developing in our times and as it affects the various disciplines of the human mind and spirit is part and parcel of the Islamization workplan. The idea was to prepare the ground for a critical and selective assimilation which could become the catalyst to the process of intellectual renewal. Meanwhile the more basic and crucial interaction which was taking place within the Muslim heritage itself would provide the setting for this fermentation. In this way, the interest in the Western heritage, and in commanding a reflective understanding of how the social and human disciplines were evolving there is not an end in itself.

... attaining a degree of reflective and critical understanding of the West from the distinctive vantage point of an equally whole, viable and self-knowledgeable Muslim standpoint makes for parity in the domain of cultural exchange and interaction. The demystification of the West through a progressive enlightenment of the Muslim mind is a condition for unshackling the Muslim psyche from the burden of a long-standing subservience and domination. It is a condition for assuming a new and worthy burden of responsibility to meet the challenge of thinking for oneself, in terms of one's own identity, and along the lines of a recovered self-confidence. On the other hand, admitting the principle of parity in the forum of cultural exchange is likely to open new horizons for the embattled West as well.

Taking the initiative to reflect systematically ... upon the West within the context of a recovered awareness and resolve on the part of Muslims is an unprecedented development ... it poses the challenge of devising the ways and means of accessing a rich and complex and a virtually unseizable whole ... Regardless of who or which team is in charge of launching such a monumental project, implementation will continue to pose a daunting, but not an insurmountable challenge. As long as the resolve is maintained and the efforts are determined, the pursuit persistent and unflagging, Muslims will steadily find their way through a cumulating reserve of experiences and resources.

The report was entitled "A Policy and Progress Report" in an attempt to argue the case of implementation by demonstration and example. It stressed the need for an integrated effort and planning and it put a premium on conceptual consolidation as the condition for effectively implementing a project on this scale. While cooperation would naturally extend beyond the circle of qualified Muslims, yet self-reliance was the cornerstone of this effort. Given the fact that 95 percent of the material needed for this project was already available in the published literature on the West and mostly by Westerners themselves, the issue was to identify that material and to know how to use it. This was one of the lessons gleaned from the preliminary feasibility surveys of the field, and the report outlined some possible criteria for selecting sources, classifying content, and evaluating material. As work on this project necessarily implicates a wide variety of efforts, individual and collective, and as it needs to address various domains and levels of intellect and scholarship, coordination and organization are vital. In this respect, the report pointed out that it was important to structure our efforts in a way that facilitated a systematic and integrated pursuit which ensured that the various inputs would be consistently related and channelled to effect the desired cumulative impact on the overall Islamization program. At the same time, it warned against the limitations of an organization that might stifle initiative and innovation in what was essentially an intellectual and pioneering enterprise. It pointed to ways in which safeguards could be incorporated in the planning stage and initial layout itself, and outlined some of the actual beginnings within the Institute's "Western Project Department" to this end.

The Premises on an Encounter

In exploring the parameters of the encounter with the West and in redefining its terms, a new beginning could be made in the making for both parties involved in the encounter, Muslims and Westerners alike. The present volatile setting may give Muslims the benefit of the initiative in this respect. Aspects of this encounter will be discussed below (chapters 5 and 6). The following remarks may serve to highlight some of the generalities which will be pertinent to that discussion.

First. The designation of the term Islamization of knowledge to a significant current in the Muslim intellectual revival calls for some passing qualification. What started out as an ambiguous and controversial appellation has come today to be part of a standard currency in circulation. Without going into the peregrinations of the term in Muslim discourse, I shall merely point out some of the lingering doubts associated with it to the extent that these might impinge on the conception and implementation of the Western Thought Project. At first glance, the designation suggests the requisitioning of a body of existing knowledge and its appropriation within an alternative valuational context to signify its legitimation to the appropriating community. In a sense, then, knowledge here implies a thing "out there" that is to be had, or acquired, and then used in terms consistent with the value framework of the Muslim community. This, however, is a denotation that has been open to question on a number of counts, not the least of which is the questionable conception and understanding of knowledge as a reified category and its confounding of the category with its forms. The resolution of this question is by no means a matter of formal definitions, but constitutes a dimension in the process of an evolving cultural movement as much as an issue within it. Suffice it here to point out these implications without passing judgment or indulging in refutations. The term has served its purpose as a focal point for stirring debate – and consciences.

Beyond any dubious connotations however, the term expresses an unequivocal conviction. The debate on the Islamization of knowledge, as Davies rightly reminds her readership,[4] is ultimately a quest for the contemporary meaning of Islam amidst the complexities of the modern world. This is also the general context for seeking to shape an Islamic epistemology and an Islamic social science. In common with all other initiatives in the contemporary Islamic revival, however diverse, the basis of our search is the consciously acknowledged need and desire to make a return to the values and principles of Islam as the starting point and objective of action and inquiry.[5]

The reflection on the West and its cultural artifacts as constitutive of the dominant global culture of our times is motivated by this concern. As such, this reflection is as much a part and a function of a modern

Islamic episteme as conceiving of an embryonic social science or as laying the foundations for a modern sociocultural entity in Muslim societies would be. Without its Islamization of knowledge referent, the Western Thought Project would be meaningless. It would be a redundancy in the incessant flow that has gushed through, impeded, expedited or otherwise, over the last century or two between Islam and the West. The point of the Western Thought Project is not to introduce the West as such to Muslims (or, obversely, Muslims to the West), nor is it by any means an endeavor to impute a legitimacy where it is not due. What is at stake in the processes of cultural exposure which permeate the globe today is not the issue of mass acculturation, but it is that of mass deculturation. This affects Muslims and non-Muslims, including those historically or culturally identified with the West. This meaning becomes clear when we consider the general and pervasive disorientation which has set in under the guise of a "postmodernity." The need is to chart out the course of a new encounter with the West, and within the West, in terms drawn from the *tawḥīdī* episteme. It is only then that a dynamic and equitable process of cultural exchange can be set at an even keel. This is what is subsumed when reference is made to the Islamization of knowledge as the premise for this project.

Second. The other general remark pertains to the historical background of the encounter with the West. If the Islamization of knowledge provides the referent and conceptual frame of this encounter, as is postulated and shaped at the level of the Western Thought Project, its context is conditioned by the accidents of a long-drawn history. If we confine ourselves to the modern encounter, we shall find that it goes back approximately two hundred years to the colonial episode, which conditioned its mode and which has structured its course ever since. Within the Muslim Ummah, this course has been characterized by an endemic tension premised on the outgrowth and persistence of two "culture species" in a predominantly deculturated environment: the assimilationists and the rejectionists. Admittedly, there was a shadowy ground between the one and the other which was occupied by the "middlers," who constituted a significant majority. It was a significance, however, matched only by its ineffectuality. The polarization between the first two groups was sufficient to secure a state of endemic cultural immobility in the Muslim world.

Against this topology, there are two ways of looking at the context of the modern encounter with the West. One is to continue to maintain one's stance from the barracks of the colonial episode; the other is to look for new benchmarks. Fortunately we do not have to look far. It is here that the current Islamic revival affords the occasion and the opportunity for new standards in reading our past and envisioning the future. More than a current benchmark, it signifies a recovery of the whole. In this way, it contrasts with the chimeric interlude imposed by the colonial episode, where the Ummah, fractured and fragmented, was cut off from its past and deluded into an illusory progress in a ransomed future. In its then dehistoricized existence, it was extended a lease on a leash. Against that contingency, the revival constitutes more than an antidote in conditioning and restructuring the terms of the modern encounter with the West.

Revival impels us to take a fresh look at the world and at our place in it. The recovery of the consciousness of the self is attended by its corollary in a reordering of our relation to others. At the same time, the situational constraints compel us to give priority to the West as the ubiquitous other – the other of our present as much as of our past – and to come to grips with the various guides in which this otherness maintains its presence (power, culture, technology; global/universal etc.). The Islamization of knowledge, as the intellectual response of the revival, qualifies the nature and mode of our reawakened responses to the West. It is at this juncture that the historical and the intellectual, or the contextual and the conceptual, converge to affect our conception of the Western Thought Project. The historicity and continuity of the encounter with the West in itself becomes the object of inquiry as well as a context for the inquiry.

Third. The Western Thought Project will need to address two dimensions of a pressing quest. On the one hand, it is a means to render accessible to the Muslim at the threshold of an epochal revival the products of the West: whether as a means of their reappropriation and their eventual transcendance – *Aufhebung* – or otherwise. One can only reflect on the meaning of the *āyāt* in the Qur'an defining the mission of the final divine revelation to humankind to adduce some affinities. One will realize that this line of reasoning, which presupposes the preservation of the most valuable and valued elements in the human legacy and their reinforcement and supersession by that which is more wholesome and complete, expresses an authentic Muslim aspiration. On the other hand, it is also the premise for assuring and completing the conditions for this revival by interpreting the modern West as the bearer of a humanistic and rationalist culture and as the locus of a contingent historical agency. This interpretation is necessary for Muslims as well as for non-Muslims in a venture which is not without its consequences for everyone in a common global setting. To the extent that there is any simulation of universality to such humanist and rationalist claims, it must be admitted that the responsibility for acting on the behalf of a common good is incumbent on all. Here, too, the inspiration for these sentiments comes from the Qur'an and the hadith of the Prophet, peace and blessings upon him.

In the school of prophethood, Muslims learn that there is no room for indifference. Witness the hadith that teaches: "The example of the one who commits a transgression and the one who is its victim maybe compared to the fate of a group aboard a ship. Some were on the top and others were below, when those who were below – tiring of climbing on deck with their buckets to haul water – got an idea: it was to bore a hole in their cabins below and obtain their water without bothering their deck inmates. In this case, if those above left those below free to pursue their ways, then surely all would perish; whereas if they checked them, then they, along with all the others, would be saved." In this kind of community, such as is envisaged in a *tawḥīdī* paradigm of knowledge, there is no escaping one's responsibility for oneself and for the whole to which one belongs. In these terms, an Islamizing perspective on the West would not see in it the other, but it would be a part of the whole to which we all belong. Again, our legacy teaches that: "Every Muslim is outposted on a vigil to preserve and safeguard that whole." There is no reason why the historic encounter with the West at a fateful juncture in the current global transition should not constitute such a vigil.

With these two dimensions of the Western Thought Project in

view, the terms of the encounter with the West can be addressed to take into account its purpose. At one level, Muslims seek to reformulate the terms of the encounter with the full weight of its historical legacy behind them. Here, the West is conceived in terms of the historically Other, and the Muslims see themselves as the contenders in an unfolding discourse which began with the rise of Islam and the earliest contacts with Byzantium and the Franks and which has continued down its meanderings into the present. This is the conventional "Islam and the West" saga which needs to be overhauled to the benefit of a more constructive historical partnership. Here, the emphasis of the Project is on a selective interpretation that is both therapeutic and propaedeutic. The priority is on restituting the terms of the encounter, as Muslims see themselves facing the West: not necessarily against it, but destined to interact with it. At another level, the Islamizing referent imposes its own dynamic in an all-inclusive discourse which sees the challenges in the temporal issues and calls for concerted and common action. Here the emphasis shifts from the participants to the grounds, and the distinction is made in terms of morality and not of history. The deference to the past in the first instance is transcended by a concern for the future. Here, it is no longer possible to speak in diffuse terms of "the West," but it is necessary to define which West is at stake in the process of grounding the discourse of the future. If, for example, it is the elements of a pagan West that are in dispute, then these need to be identified and expunged, while the elements of a theocentric humanism in that legacy could be refined and reinforced. In this sense, the encounter with the West becomes an encounter of parties to a common discourse within the West as well.

To sum up. Locating the Western Thought Project in the context of the historical encounter with the West has its imminent implications for the conception and the design of the Western Thought Project. Muslims need to take account of the West and understand its heritage in terms other than those which have hitherto been imposed upon them by the historical dominance of the West. The hope of going beyond historical contingency and overcoming a divisive and a splintering psyche can only be sought in conceptual premises which transcend such a contingency. This cannot be sought from within the dominant discourse of the West for obvious reasons. Nor can a historically constricted Muslim make a substantive appeal in the West once it is properly understood there, and such an appeal can be reinforced by a conventional and formal appeal to Muslims too. It is in this sense that the Islamizing referent pointed out at the outset can assure an element of transcendence which can make a distinctive and timely conception of the WTP venture possible.

CHAPTER IV

FURTHER HORIZONS: ISLAMIZATION OF KNOWLEDGE RECONSIDERED

Islamization of Knowledge Reconsidered

IT has been suggested that the Western Thought Project as it is at present conceived constitutes an integral element in the current Islamic intellectual revival. The implication of this proposition is that the intellectual revival is itself a vital measure for the recovery of the Muslim Ummah. We need to see in what way this recovery is contingent on a reformulation of the matrix of rationality of the modern Muslim mind and in what way this could impact on the reconstruction of the socio-cultural foundations of the Muslim civilization of the future.[1] While the substance of that reformulation and reconstruction will not be addressed here, the purpose at hand is to contour the junctures and interconnections of a vision and a process, as one possible reading and projection among others currently engaging efforts in the ummatic enterprise. The task is therefore to place the Western Thought Project within its Islamizing framework on the one hand and to reinterpret and relocate this framework within a more general optic of revival. The Islamization of knowledge addresses itself foremost to a reappropriation of the primary and indigenous sources of revival in the Islamic heritage – with the Qur'an and the Sunnah at the core – in such a way as to make that reformulation of the matrix of Muslim rationality possible. The Western heritage has invariably impinged on the Muslim past and today continues to impose itself even more onto the Muslim present. Part of the challenge therefore is to devise the terms for handling the

Western heritage as it conditions the Muslim setting. To do so, it will be necessary to assimilate the Western heritage as a whole, in its own terms at first, before abstracting the elements to be singled out for closer scrutiny. It would be well, however, to keep in mind the conditioning parameters of the Western Thought Project which place it within the more general perspective of the Islamic revival. Only by observing its place in this scheme can the work on the project hopefully contribute effectively to the revival.

A Glimpse at the Sources

As the original *Workplan* (figure 1) summing up the program and principles of the Islamization of knowledge provides one of the conspicuous landmarks in the intellectual revival of the seventies, it constitutes the natural access to relocating the Project. The sources for the revival lie deep within the Ummah, and in many ways the conception of the Western Thought Project is itself related to formative traits in both the revival and the Ummah. The Project is a reminder of how misleading it is to try to restrict the Ummah to any of its territorial – or ethnic – confines. It should come as no surprise therefore to see some of the authentic sources for the revival coming from the West.

Contrary to prevailing assumptions, the now celebrated *Workplan* was not the ingenious conception of any one individual. In every sense, it was the outcome of the intensive and consuming mental and spiritual gestations which took place within/among a group of Muslim graduates and scholars in the West during a decade which coincided with the turn of the new *hijrī* century. This group was instrumental in launching many of the grassroots institutions of the revival, which came to include the Muslim Student Association, the Association of Muslim Social Scientists (1392/1972) and, eventually, the International Institute of Islamic Thought (1401/1981). In the early seventies, Ismaʿil al-Faruqi[2] came into contact with this group through AbdulHamid AbuSulayman[3] and, together, they became part of the active spirits animating it. Its vanguard included engineers, doctors, and educationists as well as philosophers and social scientists. What this group shared in common was a belief in the need for reforming and renewing contemporary Muslim thought through reformulating and representing modern social thought from an Islamic perspective. What was novel about this plank was its option for the cultural imperative, rather than direct political action, as the most efficacious approach to galvanizing the Ummah out of its pervasive languor – the "malaise" – and consolidating its historical revival. The *Workplan*, which was subsequently developed and published as part of a manifesto of this movement, was the culmination and crystallization of this plank. In its original version, it was essentially a condensation and integration of the principal contributions submitted to the second international conference on the Islamization of knowledge which was held in Islamabad in (1402/1982) and which included original contributions by al-Faruqi, AbuSulayman, and others. Al-Faruqi was delegated by his colleagues to this maiden production.[4]

It is against this background that it becomes possible to understand the priorities and emphases as well as the strengths and the constraints which reflected on the *Workplan*. Its greatest merit lay precisely in the fact that it expressed the aspirations of a group, and this conception provided it with its pragmatic bent. The group may have lamented the situation of the Muslim Ummah; its intention however was not to bemoan its fate but to act to change it. It responded to a deep-seated Islamic conviction that Allah does not alter what befalls a people unless they take the initiative to do so themselves (Qur'an 13: 11). Neither by temperament nor by disposition was the group disposed to philosophize about this condition, and in its sense of urgency, the plan it conceived was designed for implementation. There was an implicit wariness of all philosophies and abstract theoretical forays. At the same time, the priority went to that dimension of modern knowledge which was wreaking havoc with the human and social resources of the Muslim community – a dimension hitherto ignored and neglected on the mistaken assumption that the Ummah's backwardness was a matter to be resolved by modern technology and scientific education. It was evident that a corrective focus was needed on a hitherto neglected department of Western knowledge which had found ready access in the educational and cultural media of the Muslim world and was filling the void created by the recession in its traditional legacy. The "modern disciplines," significantly the social sciences, were potential builders as

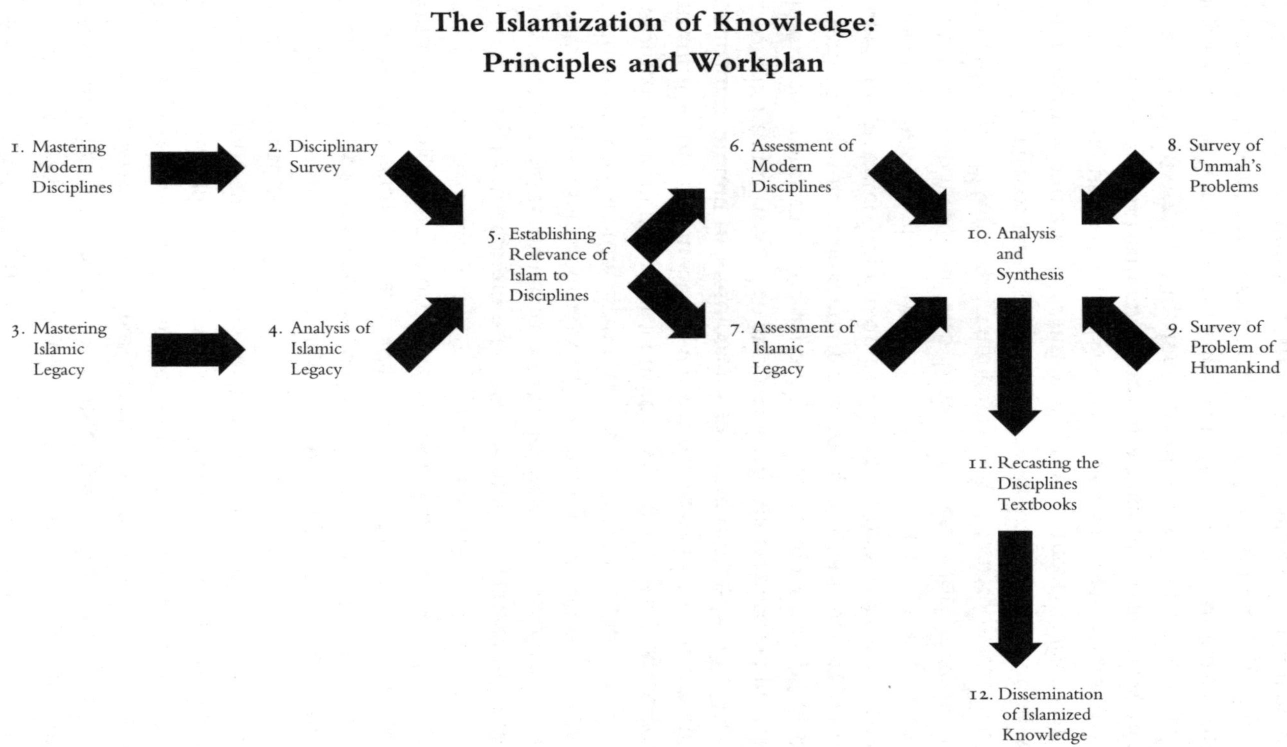
The Islamization of Knowledge:
Principles and Workplan
1. Mastering Modern Disciplines
2. Disciplinary Survey
3. Mastering Islamic Legacy
4. Analysis of Islamic Legacy
5. Establishing Relevance of Islam to Disciplines
6. Assessment of Modern Disciplines
7. Assessment of Islamic Legacy
8. Survey of Ummah's Problems
9. Survey of Problem of Humankind
10. Analysis and Synthesis
11. Recasting the Disciplines Textbooks
12. Dissemination of Islamized Knowledge

Figure 1

well as destroyers of community; it was necessary to see how these could be reappropriated in a context which would serve the Ummah rather than subvert it, as was currently the case. These were among the formative considerations which lent the emergent *Workplan* its character, as well as its strengths and weaknesses. When the International Institute of Islamic Thought was founded, it was essentially conceived as the organizational framework which would coordinate the efforts for its implementation.

The above cursory overview indicating the origins of the Islamization of knowledge *Workplan* and setting right some prevailing misconceptions in its regard is perhaps a necessary background for locating the conception of the Western Thought Project itself. It was evident that once the design was put to the practical test, problems would begin to emerge, and ways and means for effective implementation would need to be identified through efforts engaged in the field itself. It was also evident that work in the field would bring together various currents in the Islamic revival to compare notes and pool resources and expertise in order to achieve a goal which was clearly the prerogative of each and every group within the Ummah that prepared itself for assuming the tasks called for. Consequently, the Western Thought Project, as it is designed within the framework of the original *Workplan*, represents one possibility and approach to the task. At the same time, its value and merit derive precisely from its being part of a more comprehensive approach and design to securing the intellectual revival.

Charting a Vision

A series of annotated diagrams will follow to illustrate the integrality of the Western Thought Project to the general conceptualization of the revival. In the *first instance*, the Project is relocated in its original framework – as part of the Islamization of Knowledge *Workplan*. This entails a fresh reading in retrospect of a more realistic, firsthand assessment of the nature of the task at hand. The challenge shifts from analyzing the constituents of a process and breaking it down into its sequences, to synthesizing the elements of what constitutes in effect an intrinsically generated, self-propelling, and continuing process where the junctures and the parameters for its sustained progress are located.

In the *second instance*, the *Workplan* is placed in its broader context, where a renovationist optic underlies the momentum of the intellectual revival and merges it into the historical horizon of reconstructing the foundations of a *future* Islamic civilization. In the *third instance*, the Western Thought Project is brought back into focus to highlight some of the issues as they fall within its immediate precincts. To sum up the sequence of diagrams as they occur in the following pages, the first signifies a moment of *consolidation*, the second moment directs us to the *architectonics of community-building*, and the third moment returns us to a more focused stance on *topographical propaedeutics*. The idea is to capture these instances visually. The commentary itself will be secondary and will assume a truncated format of varying length and consistency.

A.
CONSOLIDATION
Islamization "2": The Sequence and Process Reviewed

The conception of *Islamization "2"* is a development and elaboration of the original *Workplan and Principles* and as such it cannot be properly understood without it. The latter had the merit of dissecting the process and identifying its constituents. It incorporated these into a lucid, programmatic format and thereby set the precedent for translating ideals into action. It also drew attention to the centrality of education to an enduring systemic reformation. The merits of the original *Workplan*, however, were also a source of weakness. Its analytic power undercut its synthetic potential, its programmatic bent betrayed a pragmatism that underrated the intellectual challenges at stake, its lucidity and clarity conveyed a deceptive simplicity, and its emphasis on education constricted and distorted the essential challenge of an Islamic intellectual reformation and revival. It also suggested some fundamental ambiguities as to whether the Islamization of knowledge was really simply a matter of more effectively adapting and legitimating an existing stock of knowledge or the search for a more radical alternative. These were some of the problems associated with the *Workplan* that needed to be addressed.

In *Islamization "2"*, the reassuring simplicity and lucidity are lost to the extent that the complexity and dynamism of an ongoing and integrated process are approximated. It is realized that this process has to begin somewhere if the "mastery of the modern disciplines" and the reassessment of the Islamic heritage are to lead anywhere, and that contrary to the initial confidence, there is no clear-cut end in view. Above all, while it is important to identify the constituents of a complicated process, the challenge is in working them together, not in isolation but integrally. The challenge is rather in synthesizing a whole, not in assembling the parts in syncretist (*talfīqī*) fashion. While education is an undeniably significant vehicle and target in any process of socialization and acculturation, let alone in any radical transformation in conceptions and beliefs, it is a link in a chain and not the chain itself. Above all, the modern disciplines and the traditional legacy are not in themselves the objects of adapting or reforming, nor do they constitute the boundaries and the ceiling for the Islamization of knowledge. These are some of the concerns which have prompted the effort to review the basic principles and directives in the original *Workplan*, and they are duly reflected in the categories and the drift of the conception projected in its review.

The objectives of the illustration (figure 2) may therefore be briefly summed up in the following points:

- To demonstrate the complexity and dynamic of the Islamization of knowledge as a continuing and integrated process.
- To rule out the mechanical and programmatic bias implicit in the original *Workplan*.
- To underline the intellectual nature at stake in what is ultimately an integral process that is best conceived in terms of an integrated circuit.
- To convey the essence and tempo of an *ijtihiādī* dynamic which is the real issue at stake in the current intellectual revival.

So much for the general observations on the operational integration of the Western Thought Project within the original *Workplan* which

Islamization "2": The Sequence and Process Reviewed:

With Inbuilt Regenerative Momentum

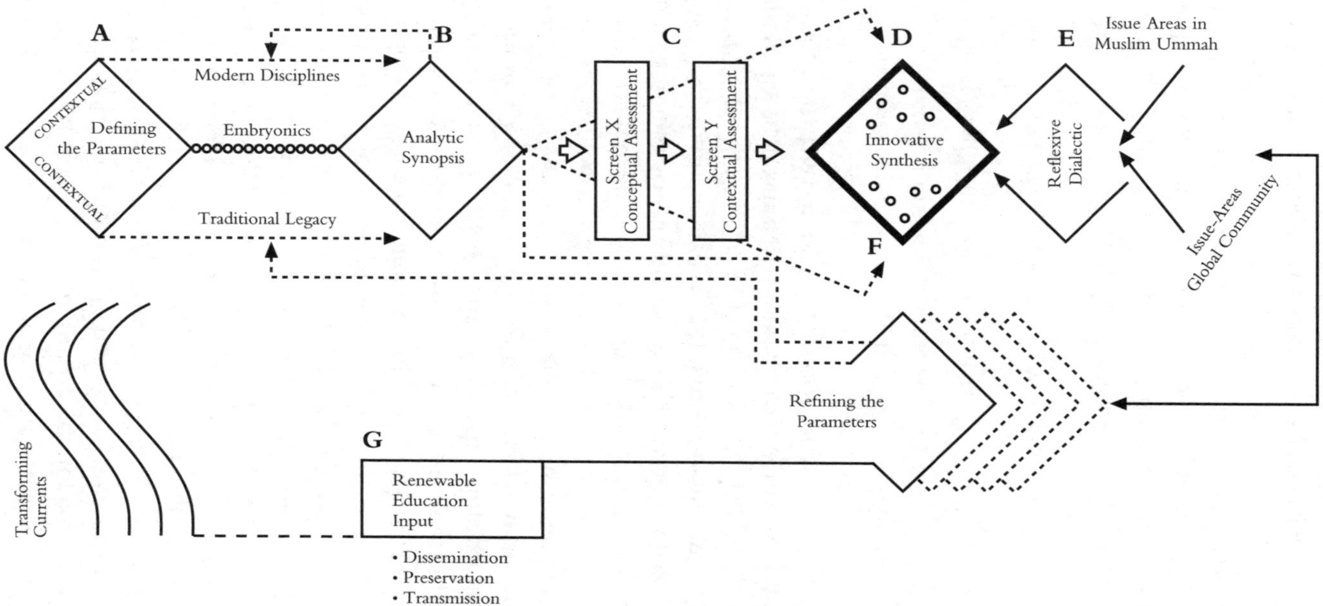

Figure 2

addressed the initial planning requisites of the intellectual revival. The themes of this reconceptualization will not be developed, since they relate to the *Workplan* as a whole. Our purpose here is simply to demonstrate that the real challenge to implementation lies in the ability to handle what is in essence an intricately involved and highly complex process which cannot be broken down to its constituent elements or "stages" without impinging on the integrality of the process itself. The Western Thought Project cannot be reduced to a phase or a stage in the intellectual revival any more than dealing with the Muslim heritage can, nor indeed is it feasible to break down the process of the revival into the stage of regurgitation from that of take-off and creativity. One may indicate thresholds and priorities for each segment of the operation, in the different pursuits individually perhaps, but the dimensions of a critical and creative venture will have to be present from the outset, notwithstanding their degree of crystallization. This underlines the importance of keeping the Western Thought Project in the general framework of the revival on the one hand and, on the other hand, maintaining an awareness of its more specific objectives which are open to periodic review and progressive refinement. The next two visuals will illustrate this. In the first (figure 3), the regeneration of the Ummah is related to its intellectual revival in ways suggested by the commentary which follows and which begins by highlighting themes of an architectonics of community-building.

B.
RENOVATION
The Islamization of Knowledge and Ummah-Building

The intellectual revival is a dimension of a comprehensive moral, spiritual, and sociocultural revival. The fact that this intellectual dimension is conceived within the parameters of Islam as a globalizing faith, community, and cultural system makes it partake of and incorporate the other dimensions. Selecting the intellectual for emphasis is a function of the diagnosis of the malaise of the Ummah and a response to the challenge of the modem historical context. In passing, it may be noted

The Islamization of Knowledge and Ummah-Building

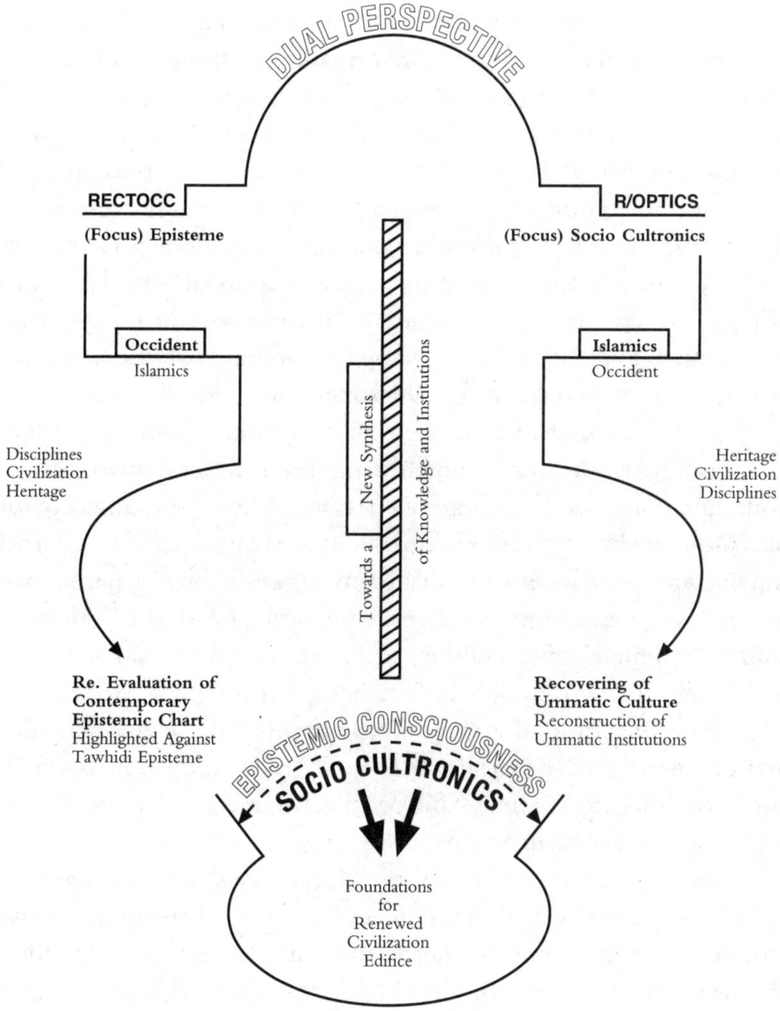

Figure 3

that the scientific age lays a premium on reason and rationality. Of all revealed religions, Islam is historically uniquely fitted for providing reason in modem times with the bearings it has lost. The *regeneration of the Ummah* is a historical process that is projected on its socio-cultural condition at any given moment. The Islamic parameters make an inner and outer regeneration not only coterminus, but they render the latter contingent on the former. The reformation of the perceptions and conceptions of the Ummah are necessarily reflected in the reformation of its social and cultural institutions, and are bound to affect its power-political foundations. Here, the relationship between the conceptual and the institutional constitutes the primary focus as illustrated in figure 3.

The Islamization of knowledge as a means to sociocultural renewal in the Ummah is the premise for reactivating its historical role as a witness among nations. The *ummah wasaṭ* (median/or middle-most community) as the *ummat al-shahādah* (community bearing witness) is essential to conceptualizing the self-perception of the Muslim community[5] (cf. Qur'an 2: 143 and 22:77-78). The recovery of the sense of historical agency in the Ummah is intellectually comprised in and contingent on activating a *renovationist optic*. This renovationist optic, *manẓūr al-tajaddud al haḍārī*,[6] is intrinsic to the Islamic parameters of the intellectual revival. Historically, Islam brought forth a nation and molded a civilization in its image (*al taṣawwur al-Islāmī*).[7] Today, the sources and the elements of the Islamic worldview remain as integral and whole and as accessible as ever before. It is part of the religious imperative to activate this view. This is contingent on an orientation and a commitment to *tajaddud*: the ideal of renovation. The Islamization of knowledge assumes this orientation and commitment in its program of intellectual revival.

Intellectual revival is part of a historical process and takes place in a historical context. While the sources of this revival are clearly drawn from an authentic Islamic heritage, its activation is neither independent of nor indifferent to the historical context. Within this heritage, the Qur'an and the Sunnah are taken as its primary note and the rest of the Muslim legacy is circumferential, to be gauged and processed as secondary sources in the light of the primary sources. This is where the relevance of the Western Thought Project emerges. The contemporary epistemic chart which impinges on the modern mind and has acquired a universality of sorts is of Western provenance. Reactivating the Muslim mind calls for interacting dynamically, critically, and creatively with this epistemic chart in a situation where being passive can only mean being submerged. Effective intellectual reactivation in the present historical context is pivoted on a *dual axis:* a vertical axis drawing on the Islamic heritage and a horizontal axis comprising contextual variables which include the presently dominant Western intellectual heritage in its various cultural formations. The dual perspective on the requisites of intellectual revival (or reformation and reconstruction) and ummatic regeneration calls for developing an *epistemic consciousness* and a *sociocultural sensibility*. These two aspects are the premise for developing the *new synthesis* which structures and informs the foundations for a renewed civilizational impetus.

The term *sociocultronics* is specifically coined to designate the architectonic dimension of the intellectual revival. It carries connotations of social engineering without overlooking the essentially spiritual and intellectual dimensions of the process. It also points to a pragmatic element or to an orientation to *praxis* in the Islamization of knowledge forum, as opposed to a philosophical or a purely theoretical intent. Again, if in current Western social thought praxis has its pejorative materialist overtones immortalized in the Feuerbachian Theses, the integrality of belief and action in a *tawḥīdī* perspective vindicates and ennobles a knowledge conducive to belief and affirms a commitment to action rooted in both knowledge and belief. In operating the vertical and the horizontal axes of the intellectual inquiry, the dual perspective which assumes a sociocultural sensibility and an epistemic consciousness is operative throughout, whether we are dealing with the Islamic heritage in a renovationist optic or whether we are dealing with the modern heritage in reevaluating the cultural topography of the Occident. The emphasis on the episteme in the one (*RECTOCC*), and on the sociocultural in the other (*R/OPTICS*) is a function of the original impetus and objectives of the Islamic intellectual revival subsumed in the Islamization of knowledge movement. The reformation and reconstruction sought is primarily intended for the Ummah, an antidote to its current stultification and sequence of historical absences. We are not out to transform the world or to change the West, but to transform ourselves. Any change that may subsequently result in the prevailing sociocultural formations and trends in the West, or in the world, will be a welcome incidental benefit.

What, it Might be Asked, are the Implications of the Above Themes for Reading the Western Thought Project?

Foremost, it may be noted that the above analytical parameters call attention to the significance of context. The Project is not to be seen apart from its conceptual format in the Islamization of knowledge movement with its focus on intellectual reformation as a means of regenerating the Ummah and rehabilitating its historical institutions. Its range and scope are predicated on this referent. In its absence it loses its rationale. The breadth of range and scope also call for diversifying and multiplying perspectives. This is necessitated both by virtue of the objectives of the Islamization of knowledge as well as in view of the complexity of the West as a civilizational/cultural entity. The Muslim intellectual encounter with the West will have to take into consideration the West of classical antiquity, the West of medieval Christianity, and the modern West with all the intervening epochal thresholds that have carried it through to a postmodernity. There is a Christian West, there is a pagan West, and there is a secular West where each of those categories is more of a prism comprising its own diversities. It is essential to capture the essentials of this multifaceted entity and to locate its diverse junctures/junctions to the extent that they permeate and shape the dominant epistemic chart which is the object of our immediate interest. The challenge posed by this breadth and diversity impels a measure of intellectual sophistication on the part of the architects of the Project. Devising a strategy to ensure an economy of access will need to be reflected in the conceptual and the methodological premises of our venture. To avoid being submerged in the welter of pluralities, we will need to work at a paradigmatic level and allow for a shifting emphasis at this level.

In view of the fact that the Western Thought Project is part of the Islamic revivalist outlook, the aspects and issues selected for examination, the priorities given, and the emphases laid in treating aspects of that heritage, past and present, will be a function of this outlook. For example, our interest will not be simply in the history of ideas, or in trends and movements, or in schools of thought and intellectual controversies; we will be just as interested in the historical setting, the implications, and the context of the interaction, transmission, or transformation of these ideas. Because the intellectual orientation in the Islamization of knowledge is related to more immediate sociocultural concerns, the epistemic focus on the Western tradition will be conceived in terms of the historical evolution and problems in this tradition.

It is the sociocultural perspective in the Islamization of knowledge that is also reflected in the priority given the social sciences (or the "modern disciplines") in the original *Workplan* and in its subsequent development. An anthropology of modernity gives prominence to this domain in the contemporary epistemic chart as the domain most immediately implicated in the formation of values and beliefs. In the socialization and the acculturation of individuals in society, they also shape and "imprint" their sociopolitical institutions. How these disciplines emerged and developed, their role, their contribution, and their limitations will have to be taken into consideration in the design and implementation of the Project. When it is realized that these disciplines set the standards for imparting the cognitive and affective orientations throughout the educational institutions in the Muslim world, and that they assume their role as substitutes for and in contention with potential Islamic sources and disciplines, the purport of this emphasis becomes evident. The new synthesis of knowledge and institutions which a renovationist optic postulates will have to call into question the prevailing authorities in any task of reconstruction. These authorities are represented at an academic and professional level in the "disciplines." Questioning the underlying structures and premises of these disciplines cannot be achieved without conceiving the totality from which they arise: namely the Western intellectual tradition and the ennabling historical context which grounds and secures the dominant paradigm. Consequently, the disciplines cannot be taken too seriously in themselves. They are the manifestation of an episteme, a disciplined compartment for ordering knowledge in society at any given moment, and they thrive on a shore of affective and cognitive values and symbols in circulation which they feed and reinforce. Any archaeology of the human sciences will tell us as much.[8] It is these values that need to be examined in their institutional and power context, and developing an original counterpoint from which to do so would no doubt precipitate their redress and eventual supersession.

The Project is taken here as a subcategory within the more variegated activities associated with the revival. In a similar summary format, the commentary will indicate the objectives, the assumptions, and the underlying themes. Given the essential unity of the suppositions which run through the Project, some repetition is inevitable. To ensure the integrity of each section and the possibility of referring to it independently of the other, I have made no effort to eliminate such repetitions where they might occur and have preferred to leave them as leitmotifs of the collection as a whole. This segment will be no exception to this rule. It illustrates how an Islamization of knowledge perspective vests the inquiry into the Western heritage and its cultural by-products with a distinctive focus and orientation. Its thrust is summed up by the denotation: *Re*viewing, *Re*evaluating, and *Re*assessing the *C*ultural *T*opography of the *O*ccident.

C.
PROPAEDEUTICS
Reviewing the Cultural Topography of the Occident: Aims and Objectives

While figure 3 sought to place the Western Thought Project in the wider context of an Islamic intellectual revival, figure 4 below closes in on its more immediate objectives and aims.

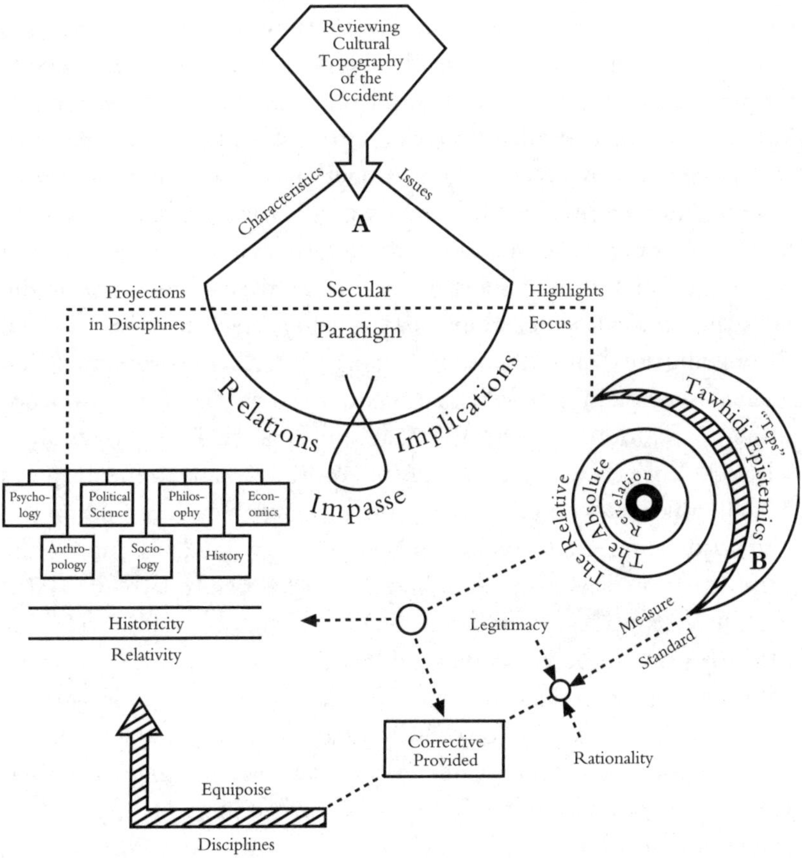

"A" to be modified, refined & redefined in light of critical orienting paradigm evolved from **"B"**

Figure 4

To spell out the assumptions of the above illustration (figure 4) constitutes a recap and a contouring of the rationale of a Project. *WTP* is part of a global Islamic revivalist outlook which takes the intellectual reformation of the Muslim mind for its starting point in resolving the cultural impasse in the Ummah. This starting point assumes a concrete and programmatic expression in the movement for the Islamization of knowledge. As the intellectual response in the current Islamic revival, Islamization seeks to operationalize Islamic norms, values, and cognitive modes in the modern historical context. In doing so, it will need to reconstruct an alternative epistemic chart drawing on its original sources. In order to do so effectively, it will need to take the measure of the prevailing/dominant epistemic chart which is patterned on the Western model. This calls for a conceptual and synthetic approach.

Modes and conceptions of knowledge are not to be confused with their constituents, or elements; the whole is not an aggregate or a sum of its parts. Conceptually, the whole can be articulated at the level of the paradigm which provides a compass for identifying and situating the parts and for analyzing them and relating them to one another. Reviewing the Cultural Topography of the Occident is a way of seeing what is involved in an intellectual encounter with the West. This is not to be confused either with the goals and objectives of the Western Thought Project, which are wider and more germane to the purposes of an Islamic intellectual revival. It might be possible to account for this distinction at a certain level by indicating that while Muslims and the reconstruction of Muslim thought remain the general goal of the *WTP*, it is the Western legacy which is the immediate object of developing the Project in the specific context addressed in the former *RECTOCC*. In another sense, understanding the elements of a Tradition, its history and its roots, and conceiving of an approach and a method is as much a function as a token of the Islamic intellectual revival. It suggests principles and proposes an initial framework for handling a complex task, principles, and a framework which is open, to further development and elaboration in the light of a maturing intellectual vision.

On the basis of the foregoing assumptions, we can locate some of the themes and general objectives of this conceptual and analytical framework. The prevailing epistemic chart postulates a secular paradigm of knowledge and being, invariably acknowledged as the worldview of modernity (figure 4). The task is to identify the characteristics of this paradigm and to retrace its implications at a theoretical as well as a practical level. This epistemic chart provides an affective as well as a cognitive dimension. How it structures relations, conceptual and sociological, and the kind of issues it raises are a function of this dimension. The impasse qualifying modern civilization is the result and reflection of the limitations/excesses of the secular episteme. Locating the secular paradigm plunges us into the heart of the Western intellectual tradition. What are the influential strands within that tradition, and why do some strands prevail and others do not? What is the nature of its flux, how does it live on to be processed and reprocessed in every age? What are the different forums for expressing this tradition, as well as its sources, and mechanisms of renewal, supersession, or transformation? The secular paradigm also structures the modern disciplines. How these latter have emerged, converged, and diverged can only be appreciated against an understanding of the nature and the development of the Western intellectual tradition. The epistemic matrix in each discipline telescopes this tradition, or at least aspects of it, just as the metatheoretical debate in the social sciences epitomizes the dilemmas and controversies in that tradition.

The paradigmatic premise in *RECTOCC* further directs attention to the integrality of culture on the one hand, as well as to the relativity and historicity of its artifacts. This is an antidote to the tendency to reify the disciplines as rational and objective, or as "given" as opposed to constructed categories. How knowledge is classified at any moment, the boundaries assumed between its different compartments, the processes of integration and differentiation, and the ordering and the parameters of the episteme are all functions of a given culture as much as its conditioning matrix. To that extent, they are likely to be historically determined. It is equally plausible to assume that different histories may claim and exact their different covalences in the culture in question if it is taken in its essential meaning as a medium and mode for moral self-realization in a temporal setting. As one postulates the structural framework for addressing the topography of the modern West, one is simultaneously reflecting on elements of a disjuncture and conjuncture with a prospective sociocultural space that is Islamic. This is why contemplating the one paradigm calls on the presence of another to the benefit of the task of reconstruction.

If the secular paradigm is an enabling premise for grappling with the modern heritage and accessing the disciplines, a complementary paradigm setting the focus on the secular paradigm and highlighting its essentials and peculiarities is the necessary Archimedean point justifying the whole exercise. This is provided by a conception of the *tawḥīdī* episteme (*TEPS*). Reviewing the cultural topography of the West can only become relevant to the Islamic intellectual revival if it is critically evaluated from within that episteme. Otherwise, there is little that is inherently novel about this survey and critique, in itself a periodic recurrence within the dynamics of the Western tradition. It is *TEPS* that assures the integrality and the purposefulness of the review of the culture and products of the Western tradition.

The nature of the *tawḥīdī* episteme, its fundamental assumptions, and how these have a bearing for evaluating the modern heritage in general and the discrete disciplines in particular is the subject of another serialized chart under the rubric of "Contrasting Epistemics."[9] The main purpose in the present chart is to draw attention to the importance of a rudimentary conception of the alternative paradigm of knowledge to assure the Western Thought Project its originality – as well as its rationality and utility. Moreover, while the secular paradigm can provide a residual critical momentum, this is essentially conceived in a deconstructionist potential. The historicity and the relativity of the dominant paradigm are brought to light by deconstructing it to its bare elements, as critical and poststructuralist schools have lately shown us. Only a *tawḥīdī* paradigm can afford that vantage point needed for breaking out of a self-imposed closure and for ensuring a critical and inclusive reconstructive momentum.

Finally, here too, one can assess the more *general implications* of the particular to the whole. Clearly, the Project calls for a sophistication in its materials as well as in its techniques. It is evident from the above cursory remarks on the need for an epistemic cartography as a delineating matrix for dealing with the congested products of an inflationary culture, that implementation calls for the highest qualifications. The task goes beyond summing up the state of the art in any of the modern disciplines to relating these disciplines to their common "genealogies," and identifying the lines that bind and wind, whether these are to be approached inductively or deductively. It is also evident that there is much that can be learned from the state of the art in the modern disciplines, as well as from the contemporary strains in Western thought, and which could be used to the benefit of reprocessing that heritage in terms of an evolving *tawḥīdī* perspective on knowledge and learning. As suggested earlier, what may be distinctively unique about this reprocessing, as suggested at the outset, is that it could lead to a potentially original and new reading of the West. What may be distinctive or unique about this reading, however, remains ultimately contingent on its Islamizing referent. On the same note, there are facts that can hardly bear reminding frequently enough. For modern-day Muslims engaged in the intellectual and cultural reconstruction of the foundations of a historically revitalized Muslim community, this reading cannot be an end in itself; it is valued to the extent that it reflects on the excellence of that cardinal pursuit.

To sum up. At the outset of this chapter we referred to a change in the matrix of rationality in modem Muslim thought as a prerequisite and a measure of the desire of self-renewal in the Ummah. The above heuristic projections direct attention to an operational mode of dealing with abstract ideas and ideals which is suggestive of a modal change in perceptions and formulations as many familiar themes in the Muslim consciousness, long taken for granted or constituting elements in the "unthinkable," now become an occasion and a milestone for critical reflection and calculated deliberation (*tadabbur*). Clearly, Muslim preoccupations with the West as it impinges on their contemporary and historical realities, and with the culture and complexities identified with modernity, do not exhaust their energies nor preclude other priorities. More central to these are the current efforts expended in redefining and reformulating perspectives on the Muslim heritage and on its substantial referents. These would ultimately reflect on the course of the various components of an overall program such as is projected in an Islamization of knowledge perspective and such as would, in particular, include the Western Thought Project. Indeed, *WTP* may be seen more as a catalyst in a process of intellectual and moral self-recovery and as a purposeful and enlightened reorientation – which is ultimately what the Islamic revival is all about.

CHAPTER V

PRELIMINARY OBSERVATIONS: TOWARDS A HERMENEUTICS OF CULTURAL EXCHANGE

Towards a Hermeneutics of Cultural Exchange

THIS chapter makes the case for an encounter with the West in terms which evoke echoes of an East/West dialogue. For a moment, the real objective of the Western Thought Project as part of an Islamization program which is primarily targeted at Muslims is deliberately muted without being lost sight of. It is an attempt to persuade the Other to come to the table and engage in a dialogue: to provide the reasons for why this is the reasonable thing to do.

In addressing the West in this way, the Muslim, as scholar and thinker, is reclaiming his individuality and position, his identity and cultural affinity, in order to give the lead and take the initiative. The first lesson in this course is to develop our communication skills. To be effective we need to know how to say what we want to say. We need to have a message to communicate as well as a motive, and we need to be able to relate means to ends in the process to assess our program and keep track of our direction. There are other needs in an effective communication situation: we need to know the important and relevant points about the Other as much as we need to be aware of who we are and what we represent. When the nature of the communication and its context are those of a cultural encounter, communication means more than a savviness in the tricks of the trade and the ways of the world: it is more than an acquisition of the essential know-how and skills. There is an important intellectual dimension to the encounter that calls for articulation and cultivation.

In approaching the Western Thought Project from the perspective of a cultural encounter in the sense to be expounded below, in the *Working Paper*, we become aware of the challenges relating to how we think and what we think, how we attempt to understand, and how we attempt to explain ourselves and others.

The other perspective on the Western Thought Project, which has already been made explicit on numerous occasions, is that of the Islamic intellectual revival. Muslim intellectuals, scholars, and thinkers are necessarily responding to the revival in terms of their trade. They want to secure a sound footing for the revival. They want to ensure that they can play a role in consolidating the winds of change blowing over the *dār al-Islām* and spurring the Ummah on to resume its place in history.

Now, whether Muslims are taking the lead in renegotiating the terms of the encounter with the West or whether they are concerned with reformulating the epistemic chart of the times along lines more consonant with the essentials of the principles and the teachings of their faith, the intellectual dimension of the challenge is paramount.

What are the elements of this challenge? These may be seen to include the following:

> *Changed Perceptions.* Muslims will have to learn to see the world differently. They can no longer assume an us/them rhetoric and affect a closure among themselves and against the world. In shutting themselves off from the world, they will not shut the world out. Doubtless, they will have to teach the Other the same lessons by their own example. Reading the modern world in terms of its globality and seeing the West in terms of its heterogeneity are aspects of the new perception. Coming to terms with their moral responsibility in a changing context should induce them to take a more serious look at how they themselves relate to their own sources and consider how they can become more genuine representatives of a legacy they pride themselves in but which, in fact, they betray in their reality. These, in short, are among the essential requisites for a changing outlook among Muslims, one which is more compatible with their authentic bearings as heirs to a prophetic legacy and as trustees of a universal message of guidance

embodying the last divine revelation to humankind. They are also its acid test.

Developing a Hermeneutic of Cultural Understanding constitutes one of the goals of the Western Thought Project, whether such a hermeneutic is conceived in terms of renegotiating the terms of the encounter with the West or in terms of consolidating the intellectual revival. While the venture is directed at understanding the Other, it is also predicated on the need to reinterpret the self. In articulating this hermeneutic, Muslim thinkers and scholars will inevitably be contributing to recharting the contemporary episteme in substantial as well as in formal terms.[1]

The essentials of this hermeneutic is that it is inspired by an Islamic ethos and is developed within the parameters of a *tawḥīdī* episteme. This can be seen in the example provided in the *Working Paper* where the rationale for the Project is set out in terms of a rational conception of the human condition as it finds its expression in the teachings of the Qur'an. This is a condition of unity in diversity, of a commonality which underlines the variety and characterizes the multiformities of a generic humanity that is conceived by a benevolent and Almighty Creator that it might "know one another" (Qur'an 49:13). The terms for this encounter of mutuality are set in a framework that carries the encounter beyond self and Other in an orientation which transcends and integrates, at the same time as it ennobles and elevates. The cue is given in the divine convocation:

> Say: "O people of the Book! Come to common terms (*kalimatin sawā'*) as between us and you: That we worship none but God; that we associate no partners with Him; that we erect not, from among ourselves, Lords and patrons other than God." If then they turn back, say ye: "Bear witness that we (at least) are Muslims (bowing to God's will). (Qur'an 3:64)

Taken in our context, the lords and patrons interposed between human beings and their Creator include those vanities and idolatries/ideologies which are adopted among groups to divide them from one another and to institute the fictitious barriers between self and Other. Meanwhile the *kalimatin sawā'* literally means the "even word," i.e., the word that is justly balanced, as well as the word that is commonly agreed to and shared by all. It may be taken here to imply a common code of reason and morality which, among other things, propose the cardinal belief in the common origins and common destiny of a human species: "created from a single living entity" (Qur'an 4:1).

It also subsumes the conviction that the ultimate source for all genuine claims of mutuality among men and women in their respective communities as to their rights, obligations, and responsibilities, lies in the infinite and absolute bounty of their Creator and Sustainer. They are assumed/and urged to be mindful of God, in whose name they demand their mutual rights of one another, and to realize that He will also be their Judge on the Day of their Return.

In an age where the dominant paradigm is blatantly materialist and exclusively temporal/secular, it is all too easy to be dismissive of this language. But a hermeneutics of cultural exchange cannot afford to do so, given the fact that such language constitutes the backbone of a living culture. Indeed, the articulation and reformulation of an episteme is contingent on recovering the currency or idiom of that living culture. So we might briefly pause to expound on the meaning and implications at hand in referring to an Appointed Day (*al-maᶜād*): "On that day shall ye be brought to judgment and not an act of yours that ye try to hide shall be concealed" (69:18). There, "every soul shall be held in pledge for its deeds" (74:38) in the certainty that "To Us will be their return: then it will be for Us to call them to account" (88:25–26). In a *tawḥīdī* episteme which inspires that cultural hermeneutic, the eschatological dimension has its implications for worldly conduct. In the final analysis, in a given historical context such claims become determinate and determining, as they shape expectations and assume form and content relative to that context. Their justification, however, and their ultimate power to bind cannot be arrogated by any one group of humanity, although they should inform the consciousness of all its members. In its moral compulsion, this knowledge can only derive from the infinity and absoluteness of its source, not its mutable channels of propagation.

The encounter with the West advocated in the present context presumes these elements and parameters of an underlying ethical and rational code of mutuality and reciprocity. It is only such a code that is believed to pave the way for dissolving the lines which divide self and Other into senseless confrontational entities and restore humanity to its essential basic oneness. The point of departure should be kept in mind through the remembrance that:

> Mankind was one single nation, and Allah sent Messengers with glad tidings and warnings; and with them He sent the Book in truth, to judge between people in matters wherein they differed. (Qur'an 2:213)

Any disputation in this regard was more likely to be provoked through selfish contumacy and needed to be exposed as such and overcome through enlightened reason. In the meantime, any residual differences which remained had to be also accepted again in the knowledge that

> Had it not been for a word that went forth before from thy Lord, their differences would have been settled between them. (Qur'an 10:19)

Such differences justified the plurality and diversity of institutions and media to represent, to express, and to contain them. Essentially, however, the underlying ethos defining interhuman and group relations should remain subject to the principle of unity and affinity among all. That realization is beautifully expressed in an assurance that carries with it a unitary reorientation that if heeded is sufficient to ensure an over riding goodwill to the benefit of all:

> Verily, this brotherhood of yours is a single brotherhood, and I am your Lord and Sustainer: therefore serve Me (and no other). (Qur'an 21:92)

It is this code which sets the tone for the auspicious title of this collection: *Where East Meets West*. Elaborating the conceptual matrix of our Project along such lines is important for consistency as well as for expediency. In this light, we are called upon as Muslims to demonstrate the merits of the *tawḥīdī* episteme as we engage in a historical process of cultural exchange in the civilizational encounter with others. The need is eventually to break the historical binary barriers and to learn to see self and Other as participants in an inclusive process which affects us all as moral beings and as members of equally purposeful and moral groups. This is necessary if we are to be effective in carrying our message through. For the moment, however, we work under existing constraints which might occasionally seem to impose their trenchant categories, along with an implicit exclusionary rhetoric, upon us. While working through them, it is important to keep our aims and alternative understanding and vision in mind, that such a constraining framework might be transformed and susperseded in the process of a dialectics of convergence attending a hermeneutics of cultural understanding.

With this qualification in mind, the closing passage of an earlier chapter in this volume might be suggestive in this regard. It explores the logic and the benefits of a profitable exchange attendant on the present phase of the great transmutation, as the terms of the encounter between the East and West are being reviewed in the scales of a changing balance of power and culture.

> ....The West can no longer monopolize the reading of its own culture any more than it can claim such prerogatives for the culture of the Other. As long as the West maintains its capacity to learn from its own insights as well as the insight of others, it can only reap the benefits of the breakdown of its erstwhile monopoly. To the extent that Muslims are willing and able to produce their version of the Western text, they will be contributing to transforming a monolithic, one track model into a diffusion model where ideas, unlike commodities and power-interests, would be enabled to create their own impact and trajectories. It is in this sense too that the assumption that the balance of modern civilization rests on culture rather than power should be understood. Ultimately, the readings of the one and the other are not exclusive, and once a perspective coming from the Islamic episteme is admitted into the global cultural horizon, it will be possible to conceive of an alternative mode of thinking which will go beyond the either/or structure to the "both and more" variant.

If the *Working Paper* which follows provides a rationale for evolving a cultural hermeneutic and outlines an agenda for this purpose, another condensed presentation which constitutes part of the occasional supplementary papers on the Project, provides a practical example and application[2] of what this pursuit entails. Obviously, this can be no more than a background and a beginning for a more general and thorough stock-taking of a situation that we see as a challenge and an opportunity. It is merely a preliminary step in setting the stage for a task which, as conscientious Muslim thinkers and scholars, we are called upon to perform.

CHAPTER VI

A PROJECT TELESCOPED: RATIONALE, OBJECTIVES, SCOPE AND STRATEGY

Rationale, Objectives, Scope and Strategy[1]

Context

THE encounter between Muslims and the non-Muslim West can no longer be conceived solely in terms of challenge and confrontation. The changed historical context, together with the trends and directions inherent in contemporary civilization, demand and allow for a radical restructuring of the historical encounter away from its conventional rigid polarities to a more accommodating and dynamic complementarity. The inducements which weigh the scales in this direction could be briefly recapitulated here. On the one hand, there are the revolutionary advances which have occurred over the past few decades in the technologies of communication, information, and in the warfare industries. In the aftermath of the massive build-up of capabilities for global annihilation and destruction, the world can ill afford the consequences of a confrontation/conflagration on the scale and intensity which have become possible. Conversely, this very logic provides the opportunity for the necessary restructuring. The politics of technology is steadily engendering a demand for a new ethics of responsibility. On the other hand, admittedly to a lesser degree and conceding the intractability of human nature, the breakthrough in technology has been paralleled by a revolution in human perceptions and expectations. It is no longer possible in the world today to defend the proposition of a naked and unmitigated imposition of wills. There are limits to one nation abusing another. Nor can nations afford to neglect the presence of one another without imperilling their own fortunes. Isolation and withdrawal are no longer a feasible alternative in a global village where interdependence is the order of the times.

In the meantime, the West has by diverse ways and means effectively managed to impose the globality of its culture on an increasingly diffident world. Yet, clearly, in the face of such diffidence this imposition cannot go unchallenged without exacting further aggravations. This realization has prompted some conscientious response on the part of concerned and responsible elements within the West itself to deplore and renounce an intrinsically unjust and unjustifiable state of affairs.

In this context, Muslim intellectuals and scholars bear a particular responsibility towards the Ummah and towards a stricken humanity at large. By drawing on their rich and immaculate heritage, they can effectively contribute to resolving some of the festering human and social inequities that threaten the globe. At the wellsprings of this heritage is the key to human renewal and social regeneration found in the instruments of the divine *tanzīl* (that which has been sent down through revelation) intactly preserved in the Qur'an and historically corroborated by the Sunnah of the beloved Prophet. These contain a wealth of radical and practical directives relevant to the predicament of modern civilization. They will need, however, to be discovered/rediscovered, articulated, and effectively communicated. In the absence of a responsible and concerned initiative to this end, the potentially vital Muslim contribution to the civilizational debacle will be aborted.

This imposes its own demands in terms of both the objective and the subjective elements of the situation. Only in a forum where a free intellectual and cultural exchange can thrive unimpeded can the necessary communication – and communicability – occur. Such a forum is not given; it is developed. Admittedly, to qualify for such an exchange Muslims must themselves qualify for dialogue. Again this qualification cannot be assumed, but must be achieved. The *hermeneutics of cultural understanding* call for a realistic and thorough understanding of the self, the Other, and the situation in which the dialogue proceeds. To understand ourselves, we need to examine our own heritage critically; to understand the Other, we need to acquire a similar critical insight into its heritage and familiarize ourselves with its culture; to understand the situation in which the modern encounter takes place, there is a need to be sufficiently conversant with the dynamics and the historicity of this relationship i.e., to be aware of its various configurations, transfigurations, the stages it has gone through, and the influences it has sustained. Understanding is the prelude to effectively acting to secure the necessary changes. In either case, a strategy is needed, whether for restructuring the terms of global culture exchange or for equipping the participants for the task.

Rationale

The Western Thought Project is our response to this challenge.[2] It is essentially conceived to make the West more accessible to the Muslim sensibility: to reduce its opacity, defuse its ambiguity, and resolve its enigmas. In a certain sense, the "disenchantment" of the West and its demystification for Muslims is the condition for a more constructive and mutually beneficient and beneficial interaction. On a more concrete level, the Project aims at a commanding intelligibility of the essence of the Western cultural heritage and it seeks to cultivate meaningful and relevant insights into the dominant themes that constitute it as a distinctive and self-substantiating tradition. The corollary to such insights is to attain a dynamic understanding of the sensibilities and the structuring forces and processes that have contributed to its shaping and reshaping as they continue to exert their influence.[3] In short, the Western Thought Project is conceived in the spirit of a desire to communicate effectively with the West by removing the internal impediments to a mutual encounter and by creating the conditions conducive to its optimal pursuit. Significantly, it signals the passing of the initiative in this regard to the Muslims. Effective communication is the prerequisite for launching a mutual learning process which underlies the dynamic of cultural encounter. In opting for the latter, however, there is a need to secure the attention of the Other: to ensure audibility as well as intelligibility. A minor digression here may serve to make a point.

To command the deference essential for mutuality, Muslims give precedence to "brain power" over "muscle power" as a counsel of principled prudence and not merely as a concession to necessity. The brain power or the intellect and reason which they invoke is tuned to a higher morality, not to an existential genetics. In so doing, they act out of the conviction that ultimately, in the human condition, there is more that unites than divides, and that underlying a necessary and imminent convergence is a rationale that mutually binds. The cultural encounter here is modeled on the aforementioned divine injunction which could be conveyed in this context as an appeal made to all those of good faith and righteous conduct who are identified as followers of revealed scripture (Qur'an 3:64; 49:13). These constitute the members of a community of conscience. They are urged to come together round an article of faith which renounces all narrow egoisms and vain idolatries and to conduct their affairs, including their public discourse, in the light of a common standard of truth which is defined in the unitarian source prescribing righteousness and to which they all essentially subscribe. This is the essence of the *kalimatin sawā'* which creates and sustains a universal moral code. This too is the ethos of an active mutuality and consonance which sets the tone for an anthropology developed in an Islamic episteme. A cursory glimpse at what such an anthropology might imply can only serve to reinforce and ground the discourse in view.

The ethos of a mutuality and consonance derives from the nature and the sources of a discipline which makes a distinctive synthesis between rationalism, in the sense of recognizing universal principles applicable to the study of all communities, and relativism, in the sense of maintaining that any community can be understood in terms of only its own identity. The synthesizing concept of both is *dīn* ... which provides the basis for any comparative study, while the concepts of Shariʿah and *minhāj* ... assure the parameters for contextualizing the universals enshrined in *dīn*.[4] In this view, a unitary, nondiscriminatory science for the study of mankind in community becomes possible where:

> ... all communities as moral domains are equivalent and are subject to the same set of conceptual principles, and are all presently engaged upon the same challenge. Whenever they existed or wherever they exist, they all enable one to reflect upon

> the implications and consequences of values and the same values will be differentially embodied and expressed by them all.[5]

The cultural encounter invoked here is further grounded in a compelling, valid, and realistic logic that premises and structures the dynamics of reciprocity as long as both parties are disposed to concede to a rationale that honors the word more than the sword. In paving the ground for dialogue, Muslims are intent on learning the techniques of the West in order to effectively convey the substance of a message intended to reinforce this rationale.

Accessibility

In the light of the foregoing, it is clear that accessibility to the modern culture and to the heritage of the West is far from being an indulgence of a sense of academic or intellectual curiosity. Seen in terms of its diverse and interrelated facets, it is a *civilizational imperative.* On the one hand, it is the condition for inaugurating and sustaining a purposeful and systematic dialogue between two cultural modes: one which is essentially *tawḥīdic* and identified with Islam, and the other which is essentially secular and materialistic and which is currently identified with the West. Juxtaposing the modes in terms of Islam and the West in this way needs to be qualified. Its binary matrix is misleading and distorts the intents and purposes of an appeal to a community of conscience which underlies the spirit of our venture. Yet, in the present context of dialoguing in an initiative taken by Muslims and addressed to their counterparts in the West, it becomes a temporary resort of convenience, or expedience, which must be hedged and contained by understanding its very limitations. On the other hand, observing the principle of accessibility has an emancipatory portent for Muslims: it is the prerequisite for breaking out of the confines imposed on the cultural forum by the dominant paradigm through continued Western domination. By addressing the latter in its own terms and on its grounds, which is what accessibility to the Western cultural mode/s secures, the limitations of this paradigm would be demonstrated. Modern Western culture too, like other human cultures, would be confirmed in its historicity and its relativity. Domination occurs when absolutes are misappropriated from the transcendental realm, to which they belong, to the mutable human realm where they can only be appropriated in relation to their purpose and their source. Where perceptions are blurred and practice abuses, then domination flourishes in a medium of absolutes, impermeability, and monopoly – an inauspicious medium which constitutes the negation of equity and undermines a forum of cultural parity and free interchange. We might briefly elaborate on this point in view of its significance for dispelling any misunderstanding.

A discourse formulated in the historically biased construct of "Islam and/vs. the West" is likely to fall within the range of a discourse of domination and exclusion. These are inauspicious grounds for any communication. By redefining the West to allow for a range of diversity, mutation, and possibility, and by dissociating Islam from exclusive ethnicities or histories which parochialize and constrain its potential openness and inclusiveness, it is possible to pave the ground for a discourse of principle and convergence instead of one that is primarily evocative of an ethos of 'discipline and advantage.' This redefinition and formulation falls within the terms and objectives of the Western Thought Project as a project conceived in the parameters of the *tawḥīdī* episteme (*TEPS*) – an epistemic field which restitutes values to their due measure.

It is important to keep that intent in mind in view of the realities which are likely to affect a pursuit, but not deflect it from its intent. The present historical conjunction between a politically powerful and dominant West makes it tempting to confound right with might, while the historical weakness and subordination of Muslims fosters their ambivalence to both power and value. In appealing to a restitution of the balance at the level of reason and intellect, there is a better chance for putting dominance and subordination in their perspective and reducing the distortions attendant on conflating power with purpose. Persuading Muslims (and others) that accessibility is feasible and worthwhile is a step in this direction. It is a step to alleviating the impact of a historical encounter from arrogance/condescension and confrontation to a prospective meeting of mutual expectations and converging reciprocities. These are qualities which would be grounded in what we shall refer to as an ethic of *marḥamah* and *taʿāruf* signifying an attitude of coming to know one another in a spirit of compassion and goodwill.

Access to the Western heritage will admit of other readings of the West by others. At the same time, it will also curtail its monopoly on a self-assigned prerogative of mis/representation by reading the Other, for the claimed benefit of the Other, and thereby assuming an unwarranted credit and authority. This is the implication of the emancipatory portent of accessibility. As this access presupposes a command of the dominant idiom, its voice will be made audible and intelligible. It takes recourse in this idiom as a medium of communication and mediation in a first stage. This paves the way for its effective contribution at a later stage. In the interval, it will at least have pushed the dominant idiom in the direction of a real diversification. Participating effectively in a global exchange, however, should ultimately go beyond limiting the dominant discourse and relativizing it, to providing it with a new impetus and new directions. On a more reserved note, one may refer to a dimension posed by the envisaged participation in the dominant idiom. Namely, the challenge to the voice coming from the *tawḥīdī* circle will be how to subscribe to the rules of the game without being caught up in them. This is a question which has been raised time and again and which is lucidly argued by others in more specific contexts.[6]

The principle of the accessibility of the Western heritage conceived in an Islamizing purview will lay the foundations for the necessary restructuration of the global cultural conservation. It will open the way to expanding the scope and the horizons of a vital discourse that will admit other parties and set the standards for a critical and constructive dialogue. In this way, the principle of accessibility to the culture and intellectual tradition of the West becomes a condition and a means for effecting the requisite changes in the environment of the East/West encounter, in addition to its evident role in equipping and qualifying Muslims to resume their historical presence and assume their moral/civilizational responsibilities.

Requisites

Handling this Project effectively calls for scholarship of a certain caliber. A premium is laid on an analytical acumen as well as on a synthesizing perspicacity in dealing with Western sources. The density and, frequently, the sophistication (or simply the underlying ambivalences) of the latter make this necessary to avert the possibility of being either overwhelmed or merely submerging passively into the text. This acumen is enhanced by an ability to balance the requisites for engagement with those for detachment. To the extent that the reader must understand the tradition from within, there is a pressing need for exerting a measure of the *Einfuhl* of Weberian hermeneutics, i.e., there is a commonsense need to evoke a certain pathos or an empathy, conducive to meaningfully experiencing the culture of the Other. A communal interchange which reinforces the cognitive dimension in its curiosity to learn about the Other with an outgoing positive affective charge *for* the Other borders on the compassionate. It may be proximated to the Qur'anic ethic of *tarāḥum/marḥamah* (deriving from *raḥmah*, i.e., mercy, benevolence, and compassion – cf. Qur'an 90:17; 30:21; 33:32; 49:13) and which, in the context of the semantic and conceptual field in which it is used in the Qur'an, appeals to a universal God conscious and conscientious bond of a generic kinship and identity within humanity.[7]

On the other hand, to observe the objective of the whole exercise aimed at intelligibility and communicability, the Muslim scholar must also keep a measured distance – hence the need for a calculated objectivity. This objectivity embraces a critical comprehension which takes into consideration the positive as well as the negative aspects of the subject culture. It calls for a discriminating sensibility in dealing with its values and concepts. It also calls for a breadth in viewing the different dimensions of the culture and a compactness in relating the parts to the whole. The sum of these qualities may be better proximated by another Qur'anic term – *ʿadl* (Qur'an 6:152; 5:8; 4:135). Taken in its literal connotations, in a context in which it is frequently invoked in the divine discourse on human guidance, it carries a double signification. Negatively, it connotes an inclination *away* from bias and away from excesses which implicitly lie at both ends of a spectrum. Positively, it connotes an inclination toward the center which is presumed to be the ground of truth, the "just," of probity/integrity: the pivot of an intellectual and moral uprightness and rectitude as against one of deviousness and deviance. This is identified as *istiqāmah* (Qur'an 11:112; 42:15; 41:30; 9:7; cf. also 25:67), which is the logical sequel and corollary of *ʿadl*. Such is the ethic of justice and integrity. More than the idea of "objectivity," which presupposes a questionable binary matrix and a reified rationality, this is what is needed to inform and reform the desired scholarship. The originality of a Muslim reading of the West is contingent on this balance between the elements of *tarāḥum/taʿāruf* and *ʿadl/istiqāmah*. In the dominant idiom, it calls for observing the proportions between "empathy" and an "objectivity".

Beyond temper and modality, this balance between engagement and distance is thus reinforced by and reinforces a kind of scholarship which is substantially grounded in an Islamic epistemology. This is essential if it is to handle the subject culture effectively in a framework reconciling distance to engagement. In the absence of this basic grounding, the critical and discriminating aptitudes associated with the objectivity essential for the task will be impaired. Conversely, keeping a calculated distance does not signify hovering in the void. Perhaps we can further illustrate the importance of "solid grounds" in the process of cultural openness to the Other by reversing gears and reviewing the alternative.

In the event of a random, dispersed, or compulsive encounter with the cultural West, the outcome is more likely to be counterproductive. A confirmed sense of inferiority, no matter under what guise, is bound to negate any opportunity for an equitable meeting of cultures. A one sided deference to the dominant culture, for instance, carries with it the undercurrents of a persistent mystification of the West and ensures such an inferiority. Nullifying the principle of parity in the relationship between the two cultures, with their respective heritages, erodes the prospects of global restructuration.

It would instead confirm the existing hegemony with its inherent antagonistic and antagonizing polarities to the detriment of alternative possibilities. This decentering, fragmenting, and dispersing impulse, or indeed, this diffuse quality of a random contact, has in fact dominated the encounter of an earlier generation that had opted for a window on the West. Yet, they only succeeded in provoking deeper reactions and engendering a greater rigidity in cultural attitudes. The resulting rift and cleavage in the ranks of Muslim intellectuals was not alleviated in any measure by the attempt to gainsay and to deny or to minimize the impact of the prevailing rift between the contending cultures either.[8] The rift has to be addressed as much as the cultures in question. It is this situation which has inspired present initiatives in the Islamization program to plan for a Western Thought Project and to take a more serious and open attitude to the West and its legacy.

The scholarship on Western thought ventured into from an Islamizing perspective is inherently engaged in laying the foundations for a more hospitable and tolerant cultural setting that ineluctably admits of other submerged voices. As the potentially enriching contribution of the Islamic heritage reemerges, an effective articulation of the Islamic worldview becomes a distinct possibility. It would also be an important step in redressing the prevailing imbalance in the global medium of interchange and in paving the way for an optimal measure of cultural parity to the benefit of all the parties concerned. In this sense, the conception of the Project could be seen in terms of a bold and innovative blueprint aimed at effecting a cultural breakthrough. Much remains to be done, however, in defining the techniques and arenas of cultural interaction and in refining the scope and perceptions of such a scholarship.

Scope

At a more general level, the needs of such a scholarship could be addressed in terms which further add to the prospect of the success of the project as a cultural enterprise on the scale envisaged. The Western Thought Project calls for a fair grasp of the nature and processes involved in cultural understanding. Of the few works that have directly addressed the issue of cultural exchange in the context of Islam and the West, the work of Norman Daniel comes to mind.[9] This and other similar works could provide a tangible starting point in a wide-ranging but often a highly abstract field. Muslim scholars will need to cultivate a sensitivity to the issue of cultural dynamics and cultural affinities on both sides of the spectrum and they will have to conduct their inquiry fully alive to its more profound implications. On the other hand, a more intimate knowledge of the techniques of intercultural dialogue in general would be useful. These could be adopted at certain junctures of the interaction with the Western heritage with a view to locating convergences, or expanding common ground and bridge-building to promote a cause or to bring home a point relevant to the general platform of cultural Islamization. In the one case and the other, a familiarity with the processes of acculturation would be an advantage. In locating the general requisites for the Project in this manner, one is evidently also pointing out some of the thematic sources in the literature which should be relevant to Muslim scholarship in the field.

More specifically, an authoritative familiarity with the Western heritage requires that we define our objectives with an eye on the conditions for their optimum realizability. This calls for expanding our heuristic vistas to a range of literature that might not ordinarily have engaged our priorities. Works on the intellectual heritage or on aspects of culture which are conceived in different contexts and for different purposes may well serve to highlight some of our own objectives and enhance our susceptibility to such conditions as would promote our ends. The way in which we handle such works, our manner of investing the points of contact we recognize, is just as important as diversifying and extending the range of literature. The products of cultured and cultural think-tanks located the length and breadth of the strategic intersections on the Western chart of knowledge and intellectual capital may at times be tangential to our immediate concerns. To the extent that they provide us with a fund of accumulated experience, they will serve to boost our own limited reserves both on the human and the temporal scales. A case in point is the monumental venture into the intellectual legacy of the West which was undertaken by Mortimer J. Adler and others and which resulted in the series of sixty volumes on the Great Books of the Western World introduced by the *Synoptican*.[10]

As the focus on the Western heritage becomes more explicit, the strategies of handling the Project become a matter for urgent consideration. This engages us at a more concrete level with given arenas that will open up our access to the heritage and crystallize the scope of the inquiry. From the outset, we will need to address certain issues and decide on the priorities. The following is a suggestive itinerary that bears further scrutiny. In spelling out the parameters of the ground to be covered, it can only enhance focus and orientation in planning for the implementation of the Project.

- What are the sources of the Western heritage? What are the specific traits and contributions of each?
- What course did the evolution of this heritage take? Can we locate the nodes of this evolution in formative periods and critical junctures? What were the factors which influenced this course and ... in what direction were these influences exerted?
- From another perspective, can we identify the landmarks in Western thought and patterns of evolution in terms of epochs and issues – and "epochal thresholds?"[11]
- With slight variations on the above themes, can we ascertain the dynamics of Western culture in a pattern of continuity and discontinuities ... the patterns of preservation and transmission, or the cycles of production and reproduction, generation and diffusion?
- What are the different configurations of the Western legacy? Conversely, how does the latter percolate through the different layers of the culture and how is it projected in the disciplines of knowledge?
- On the intercultural level, diverse questions could be raised. In the dynamics of cultural exchange, the emphasis can be laid on the encounter with Islam. What were the stages, levels, and modalities of this encounter?
- How did the Muslims react, respond, or interact with the ideas and the heritage of the West? More to the point, perhaps, how did the West present itself to Muslims and to others? Can we devise categories for this encounter: i.e., projection and self-image vs. reflection and response?
- With a slight shift of emphasis to the context of the encounter, it is evident that the Western cultural ethos and the heritage percolates unevenly into the Muslim eco/psychosphere. What are the arenas of cultural encounter to be examined?

- In examining cultural influences, we could provisionally distinguish among three different levels or arenas in the cultural encounter: a civilizational (institutions); a cultural/intellectual; and an educational (specifically curricular content and discipline – classification).

The above ennumeration by no means exhausts the possibilities for exploring strategies and means for designing the project. It is suggestive, however, of the many questions which could be raised and which could provide useful frames of reference for researching specific topics. The range of the latter is as vast and varied as its subject matter. Researching the Western tradition with an emphasis on the nature, course, and forms of its encounter with our own heritage and history as Muslims can initially be organized around historically structured nodes or thresholds such as the following themes would suggest:

- The Graeco-Roman and biblical roots and sources of the Western tradition and how these have been repeatedly projected and processed in the different strands of the Western tradition – (Anglo-Saxon and Continental, or German, French, English, and American); how they have impacted on the modern West and its culture; and conversely, how Muslims are inclined to view and distinguish these sources to the extent that they do or may have done in the past.
- The Andalusian heritage: its significance and its potential implications for a Muslim reading of the encounter. Bringing it into focus can enhance an understanding of the patterns and consequences of the transcultural interaction between Europeans and Muslims both in the past and in the future.
- Renaissance, Reformation, Enlightenment, and Revolution, or the epochal moments in modern European history: a reassessment of their meaning and implications from a Muslim perspective – whether in terms of experiences specific to the European setting or in terms of their actual consequences and implications for Muslim history and society.

The scholarship of the Western Thought Project would be expected to dwell on the above themes directly and to develop original interpretations. But it would also be a reflexive scholarship and it could go beyond the historical to the substantive approach to the issues. In this case, the focus could shift along the following lines:

- Surveying and assessing the current scholarship on the above themes, both Muslim and occidental. Identifying trends and characteristic patterns and tracing influences and genealogies in the field. This would include an inquiry into the field of orientalist scholarship and its critics.
- Contrasting and comparing respective perspectives in the two traditions, the Islamic and the Western, on knowledge, ethics, culture, philosophy, religion, history, and civilization. Their implications should be sought with reference to the modern context.
- Identifying the challenges and problems in the contemporary episteme both in the Muslim Ummah and in the West. Central issues could be located and addressed, i.e., the relationship between reason and revelation, reason and ethics, values and sciences, or power and responsibility, etc.

EPILOGUE:
RETRIEVE AND RENEW

Retrieve and Renew

THE discourse between East and West is a task which cannot be relegated to future generations. It has already begun within our generation. Such projects as the one which has been the subject of the present collection is merely an illustration of the direction in which Muslims today are thinking. Writing from within a *tawḥīdī* perspective, carrying the legacy of the Muslim past, and with the burdens of its present in view, it was only natural that the priority and the emphasis have so far been given to rousing Muslim scholars and thinkers to their responsibility towards the Ummah. Their counterparts in the West must evidently also share in a common responsibility of clearing the horizons for a future global moral order which is inclusive and humane. It must embrace everyone and be equally accessible to all peoples and cultures indiscriminately.

Only a century ago, such prominent figures proclaiming their affinities and allegiances to the Enlightenment could equally boast a misconceived arrogance in their claims that the future belonged to Europe alone.[1] It is not surprising that in the presence of such paradoxes where reason and bigotry coexist the twentieth century would live through the wanton excesses which would leave everyone the poorer in their humanity, not only Europeans. However, man is conceived by his Creator in dignity and a divine spark of hope must forever burn in his soul. The twentieth century has also been something in the way of material achievements and more by way of aspirations to higher elevations of an englobing morality. Dialogues and trialogues have been taken up with varying degrees of commitment and consistency among the different peoples and traditions. They constitute the cultural venue of a politically self-conscious age. This is one area upon which intellectuals in the East and the West need to reflect in earnest.

A cultural hermeneutic conceived in the spirit of a *tawḥīdī* ethos, impartial and at the same time engaged, could provide the corrective and the measure to safeguard against complacency and to spur on a benevolent sense of equity in the regard for others. It would be impartial in terms of its distancing from contending egoisms, its "bracketing" of the self-centered impulse; it would be engaged in its commitment to the pursuit of the truth and its fulfillment in history: in the "worlding of the world." To take up the lead provided in the prologue, the only test and warranty of integrity in observing this intent lies in the source and premise of its inspiration. The intent begins with the Qur'anic recollection and knowledge that:

> Mankind was one single nation, and God sent his messengers with glad tidings and warnings; and with them He sent a book in truth, to judge between people in matters wherein they differed; But the People of the Book, after the Clear Signs came to them, did not differ among themselves except through selfish contumacy. (Qur'an 2:213)

Despite their differences, people were meant to strive to "know one another" (Qur'an 49:13) and to use these differences as the gauge of their complementarity and as an access to a purposeful and compassionate mutuality that went beyond the mechanics and the impositions of functional and contingent interdependencies. To do so would require of them, however, a modicum of convictions and a modified self-perception that took its cue from another reinforcing Qur'anic injunction:

> Verily, this brotherhood of yours is a single brotherhood, and I am your Lord and Sustainer: therefore serve Me (and no other). (Qur'an 21:92)

In world politics, where the price of power without responsibility has soared in modern times, the turn of a new century seems to promise new crossings as the walls which have long divided crumble.

Symbolism is rife, and nowhere more so than in the celebrations from the Berliner Schauspiel on Christmas Day playing Beethoven's "Ninth Symphony" which was relayed by satellite across the globe. There the ode to brotherhood was transfused into a hymn to human freedom. This optimistic surge might be true for the spectacle on the Western front. There, one version of an East/West divide which has fractured the Northern hemisphere during much of the outgoing century, and which in the process had for long imperilled a shrunken globe, seemed at least for the moment to be giving way. A kind of intoxication seems to be taking over as individuals and peoples emerged to reassert their long denied God-given rights. It is this resurrection of a persistently distorted and a stubbornly dodged source of human morality which seems to be taking the historical West by surprise.

The transformation of totalitarian regimes in the face of popular pressure is more than the ideological triumph it is taken to be by its enthusiastic liberal contenders. Beyond the much vaunted principles of political freedom there are even more elemental values which are at stake in the present global effervescence. The perennial quest for dignity and spirituality peaks at the height of a materialist age. It takes a person of Vaclav Havel's sensitivity and humaneness to remind his baffled and admiring audience in the West of the persistence of an "inner realm of truth" which has sustained his nation through the trials and rigors of an automated and perfected totalitarianism in a Communist regime that to all appearances ruled indomitably for over half a century. Havel is of course that Czech playwright, poet, and politician who rose from dissident to president in one of the more providential turns in this century.[2] It is to be hoped that this aspiration to an innate spirituality which extends to the public realm will not be sacrificed at the altar of another variant of the materialistic vice embodied in the consumerist ethic of the liberal West.

This quest for an inner realm of truth, one might add, is perhaps just as evident within the bounds of liberal democracies too, where the urge to affirm a moral order is at hand. There the virtues of political freedom fall short of assuring the means for overcoming a host of other problems afflicting modern communities around the globe. The need to look beyond politics, if not to turn politics itself into a paradigm for salvation, is very tempting. The historical West, while politically vindicated and technologically unsurpassed, remains a lone and proud victim of its own virtues and accomplishments. Others might be inclined to be less charitable and call a spade a spade. Defiance and rebellion – (or is it arrogance and self-delusion?) – is after all a Promethean patent with which some will gladly identify. Nonetheless, one lives in history and realities that need to be resolved impose themselves.

The need to transcend the claims of a permissive society and to curb the effects of an unbridled individualism seem to be persistently offset by a contentious ethic of cultural relativism. The modern West takes pride in its rational liberalism, yet for all its reverent skepticism it is not at all sure how it can handle its growing human problems. The demand to do something about values that are turning into vices also grows. If this demand is more often articulated in terms that are more social and cultural, yet they frequently boil over into ominous incursions in the political arena. Although they assume decidedly less dramatic form when compared to the events in China's Tiananmen Square or at the Berlin Wall, they are nonetheless historically portent in the Toynbee sense. The spectrum of American anxieties on the eve of a new decade and at the threshold of another century provides eloquent testimony to this effect. A catalogue of nagging issues tests the mettle of its intellectuals as much as the boundaries of its moral and political order. Drugs, sex, abortion, child abuse, pornography, a permanent underclass of homelessness and underprivilege – these are among the social plagues of the day which constitute items of priority in that liberal order. The cultural resources of the Western tradition are strained to the limit, and the public debate which touches on such issues as ethics and public policy, or the relations between church and state, does more to disclose the strains in this tradition than to relieve them.

This again is an area which stands to gain by promoting such initiatives and research as those expressed in the Western Thought Project sponsored by the advocates of Islamizing knowledge. "Islamization" as the preface to the *Roundtable Collection* suggested, is hardly a program for wholesale conversion or for proselytization. Rather, it is a universal summons to learn and to reeducate the self which begins with a rational appeal to Muslims themselves. This appeal stresses the need for reintegrating a core of pristine values that are universally accessible to everyone into the matrix of modernity through its information and education networks. As these values are recovered and reformulated, they are also woven into the basic grounds of knowledge and they can come to inform techniques, technologies, policies, and institutions to the benefit of a wide public.

The human and moral problems in the advanced West constitute an area which suggests to all concerned that it might be salutary to open up to other perspectives on the world and on life. Admittedly, a perspective coming from a *tawḥīdī* worldview might have something to contribute to resolving problems which, by virtue of modernity, can rarely be confined to any one part of the globe. With a clearing made in the cultural space of the West, one could hope for a turn towards a *tawḥīdī* episteme. To the extent that such an episteme is admitted into the intellectual and cultural horizons of a discourse, which would be carried beyond the current elated idiom of a *glasnost* politics, a welcome access could be assured to the global reserves that would shore up a new moral order. But this could only occur if the obsession with power and power politics which is so rampant in the dominant forums of our day were to be scaled down to its proper proportions. Yet, here we come to the crux of the matter. The very word "proportion" seems to be a term which has lost its meaning in an age which can only see itself in an implosion of refractions as it desperately gropes for both content and direction.

"Nothing in excess, measure is best, know thyself!" So the echo sounds of the delphic oracles of a bygone age which seems to have been entirely lost to the consciousness of a present confounded in its self consuming immanence Modernity. This is an epoch which was spawned in the West and now credibly threatens to engulf the globe. Yet it makes sense to recall a timeless exhortation of natural prudence, confirmed in divine revelation, handed down over the generations and understandable to all, in both East and West. It needs to be taken seriously on the agenda of any future encounter between East and West which presumes to address the future ecology of a moral global economy. In its absence there can be no "New World Order" in a shapeless post modern age which is dawning on both East and West, and which is seeking its shape. All the same, the boundaries are more than ever becoming those

between a reason enlightened by faith and prudence and a blind reason intoxicated by its own excesses and want of restraint. This is what an outgoing epoch is teaching posterity, although its own generation is seemingly impervious to the lesson. When the individual has become a measure unto himself, the community dissolves: or at least, its matrix is severely undermined. In the meantime, there is nothing that can secure the individual either against his own excesses. In forgetting their Creator, their origin, and their destiny, God has made them oblivious of themselves (Qur'an 59:19).

This is the real implication of the controversies of our times, whether they are of global vintage like the Rushdie scandal, or whether they are more local eruptions like the Cincinnati Museum court case deciding on the fate of the Mapplethorpe collection.[3] The one and the other, each in its own way dramatizes the central issues at stake. In the soul searching they provoke, the thin end of the wedge is broached in an attempt to deliberate on what constitutes "art" and what pornography, and on where the lines, if indeed any, should be drawn between the rights of the individual and those of the community. It was only the politicization of the first of these two issues, the Rushdie affair, and its interpretation within a saturated ideological setting which obscured its real dimensions.[4] These could only be understood in terms of an unbounded and unrestrained effusion/implosion which undergirds the modern secularist culture. In an event which threatened to cloud the historically dense and fragile horizons between the Orient and the Occident, and to stir dormant passions in the saga of "Islam and the West," there were other factors confounding the benighted affair. Foremost was the pervasive impact of a market-oriented media which was typically tempted into publicizing a "death defying novel" to thousands of gullible and well-intentioned buyers. Numbed by the dulling banalities of a boring age, there exists in the West a ready public which is all too eager to join a crusade, even if only for the excitement offered and the opportunity to vent one's pent-up sense of righteousness and frustration. Here again, another valid lesson of our times was lost in the fray. There was no longer an East "out there" to be ravaged, romanticized, taken to pieces, revelled in, phantasized, or exorcised. The East was now within the West and, in a way, it was as much a part of it as the

West, in its globalization, had become of the East. That was reason enough for all sensible men and women of goodwill to come together to defuse the spurious and vicarious spark. This thought conduces to another observation which would not have intruded here had it not been for its implications for an East/West encounter.

Indeed, to many thoughtful Muslims who live in the West, as well as to many concerned Christians and other liberal thinkers who are honest with themselves and courageous enough to admit it, there are many perplexities on the horizons that need to be cleared. Many are trivial incidents blown out of all proportion, whether out of malice or more frequently out of ignorance, misunderstandings, misperceptions, misguided analogies or any other contortion. At about the same time, like the Rushdie affair in the Anglo-American world, another minor happening across the English Channel triggered off tensions there. An administrative interdiction by the French authorities banning the veil/headscarf from public schools was proclaimed in the name of safeguarding "secular freedoms." Such incidents were bound to raise doubts about the genuineness of the liberal credo. That these incidents coincided with the sweeping developments in the Continent and throughout the globe at the close of an eventful decade, these questions were all the more compelling. At the height of their vindication it would seem, when their proud mentors were debating the Hegelian thesis of "the end of history,"[5] the celebrated ideals of the liberal polity seemed also, ironically enough, to be at their most vulnerable. Beneath the surface pomp and luster, frustrations festered and anxieties churned at the fringes. Equivocations in the standards of freedom and of rights threatened the public peace as much as troubling many private consciences. How free was freedom? Freedom for whom and freedom to do what? Whose human rights, and who qualified for the designation "human"? With a steadily growing community of Muslims in the West, both of indigenous stock and of emigrants, these are questions that will have to be addressed to satisfy an innate sense of justice as well as civic entitlement to equity for all.

Whether in their historical *dār al-Islām* homeland in the East or in their new and adopted home in the West, Muslims are essentially struggling with the questions of identity and community in an environment that needed to be sensitized to both. For such Muslims, however, there was not a shred of doubt about the immutability and the contemporary vitality of the divinely revealed principles which to them, more than an article of faith, constituted their reason for being. The question was how these principles could be instantiated in a changing time and clime: it was a problem of form and contemporization, not one of content or of direction. The Islam of history that Muslims have lived in the more recent and more distant past, many felt, was not necessarily that of the future; nor, as they well knew, were the boundaries among communities exclusively geographical or ethnic; they were primarily and above all moral. The real task and challenge, as many a self proclaimed theocentric humanist too would readily concede, was how to evolve a global architectonics of a community that was both free and moral, and how to launch this project from within the West itself, from the lion's den and the eagle's nest. Much would depend on common people's attitudes and on public policies towards the multiplying circles of "pluralisms" there.

The pressing question, however, would remain the same one that has periodically resurfaced in the great conversation in the West: Could a moral order be worked out without degenerating into either tyranny and dogmatism or nihilism and licentiousness? Could the extremes in an inherently oscillating culture be avoided? For Muslims there is no doubt about the possibility for such a golden mean, as such a possibility constitutes their perception of what their test and witness in this world is about. The challenge, however, lies in how to strive towards instantiating an intrinsically realizable ideal. More to the point in the present context, the question was how the encounter with the West and from within the West could be developed within the framework of a *tawḥīdī* ethos in a manner that would contribute to resolving some of its perennial self-inflicted dilemmas.

Given the "global village," where a century's technological accomplishments have dissipated the physical distances between communities and cultures, the East/West encounter has become doubly imperative: not just to avoid the consequences of such potentially explosive misunderstandings, but also to deliberate together and to redefine the bounds of rationality and the meaning of community. This is a task which challenges a common endeavor to bring together values and good will as well as the power to give them substance. Such a task cannot be left to the West alone to decide on and bring about, for if the West has no want of power, it is demonstrably powerless to save itself on the scales of morality. While it is evident that no culture can flout morality, yet it is equally true that history is strewn with the records of civilizations that have lost out in the wake of abortive searches in pursuit of their elusive ideals. In the meantime, if it is left unsubdued in its directionless and contentless will-to-power, the West, under the delusion of its monopoly on progress and right, can only destroy itself and others. The idea is that there still remain strong pockets of morality and conscience in the modern West, particularly in the transatlantic New World that is rapidly ageing, and that these need to be reinforced and shored up. At the same time, the Orient, as the historical fount of values and morality, cannot afford to indulge its complacencies and to simulate a disdain for power without marginalizing itself from history. But then, in its own carelessness and misconceptions, it will be guilty of partaking of an end to all history in the very real and tragic sense, its own history and that of others, in a world that can ultimately know of only one history for a common humanity. This is where the prophetic ethos of a joint sense of responsibility for the fate of our global ecology comes alive.

It would not be unseemly at the close of these reflections to paraphrase and briefly dwell on the gist of a parable cited earlier as a reminder of this ethos.[6] The victim of folly and its perpetuator, it is held, are equally responsible for their plight in an affliction that is visited upon all in our planetary ship called Earth. If those who at one end see fit to deplete its resources or abuse them in a manner that suits their own selfish temporal interests, regardless of others who share with them the earth at a given moment or in the future, and if those others are too indifferent or complacent to act in time to check abuse, then all would eventually perish. The limits of moral responsibility for the public good are set.

What we refer to as the prophetic ethos also inspires dialogue and encounter across cultures, and it might be rendered as a code which balances the elements of personal and public responsibility in such a way as to assure the dignity and moral well-being of all. As a rejoinder to the theme of joint responsibility, it might be pointed out that each individual and group may ultimately carry the burden of one's own deeds in an ethic where "no soul shall bear the burden of another" and where none shall be taxed beyond their capacity – and where, moreover, each group is judged in terms of its own mandate and not that of another.[7] Carried into the realm of responsibility for the action of others in the task of worlding the world, this might evoke its echoes in a variation on a theme from an analogous tradition. "I am not my brother's keeper" cannot simply be countered by its obverse. Rather, the well-meaning insistence that "I **am** my brother's keeper," which could open the way to abuse and transgression, would need to be qualified with the remembrance that "My brother is also my keeper, as long as neither of us legislates for the other, and as long as we both deliberate together in implementing a code revealed to us by our common Creator and Benefactor."

A *tawḥīdī* episteme which embraces that ethos sees the parties to encounter and dialogue in a relationship that transcends their mutual obligations and reciprocities to reach out to their originating, mediating, and arbitrating source. Accordingly, the rationale against a morale of selfishness and indifference here was as simple and practical as it was morally salubrious. At the same time that it inculcated a sense of commitment and purpose to secure a cohesive moral community, it safeguarded it from degeneration into an arena of self-righteous tyranny by maintaining the proportions between the personal and the collective, the internal and the external, the immanent and the transcendent. The essential point to note in such a community is that there is no escaping that sense of moral responsibility for oneself and for the whole to which one belongs. This point is only reinforced by the knowledge that history, i.e., the lapse into temporality and the sheer passage of time is no excuse for forgetfulness.[8]

Muslims can play an axial role in an epoch of transitions as they deliberate on their own destiny. Historically, this role has been conceived in terms of retrieval and renewal. Today, retrieval and renewal are a burden that they must share with the Other in confronting the challenge of the times. To retrieve and renew is this 'double-barrelled' quest which confronts all those who live in the modern world: it means to rediscover, to remember, and to recover their common values and it also means to renew their common life on a shrunken globe as they reverse optics and come to see their planet Earth in the perspective of another epochal moment in cosmic history as it is revealed through the eyes of the Hubble telescope. If anyone is conceivably more qualified than another in taking the lead on this journey to renewal, then it is surely those who are middle-most to the encounter: those who belong to both East and West by virtue of their common allegiance to the Lord of the "two Easts and the two Wests."

It might be recalled in this context that the West has frequently seen Muslims in ambivalent terms: at one moment Muslims are seen as apart of that exotic Orient – out there, on the other side, the fabled and foibled other. But, more frequently they are seen as an extension, a projection, or a perversion of the West itself – another instance of a Christian heresy that has to be brought back into the fold – or exterminated. Only rarely is that flicker of an intuitive sensibility stirred to suggest to the few that experience it that somewhere in that extension of self, in that "continental shelf," lies the key to a magnanimous reconciliation that lies at the heart of the Western odyssey from classical antiquity through modernity. This reconciliation will have to be one that starts from the self and stretches out to embrace the Other. Those who can conceive of such a vision and its realizability are, indeed, the few whom the inspired Muslim theologian and philosopher of the sixth century *hijrī*, al-Ghazālī, referred to as "those from whom God does not denude the world" and who are, as he explained, to be found in every culture and throughout time.

Little is it realized, however, how the "middle-most community" which constitutes the Muslim norm is defined by a vertical and transcendent compass that assigns the unitary orientation to all of mankind in terms of its single origins and its ultimate destination. This is the perspective which inspired the trialogue of the Abrahamic faiths advocated by al-Faruqi as chairman of the Islamic Studies Group at the American Academy of Religion. With this, we might end on a very pragmatic and down-to-earth proposition on a somewhat more mystical and sublime note.

The middlemost community is a global ecumenical community, a universal brotherhood in the full sense of the word; it owes its character and designation to the direction in which it sets its face: its *qiblah*. Every Muslim knows what the *qiblah* is. In his prayers five times a day he sets his face to countenance a source and direction round which the hearts of millions of his brethren converge in humble devotion. But in the encounter with the Other, the significance of the Abrahamic sanctuary, that time-honoured House of God which beacons to all His thirsting bondsmen, will need to be communicated on the plane of a paradigm. In this context, the *qiblah* could be transfused symbolically in terms of an interiority that stretches outward to the infinite. Or, obversely, it could be perceived in the heart of the devotees of a world of truth and light, in terms of a transcendence that is projected in a visible center of finitude where it is instantiated and to which all who care to turn can palpably relate. Whichever way it is defined and communicated, the *qiblah* ultimately signifies that nodal point which reaches to the invisible depths of the core of our humanity as we seek to internalize within our consciousness and our consciences the values that can save our common history. The direction of the shaping/reconstructed middling global moral community as it comes to prevail over the derelict dichotomies that artificially divide, stretches beyond itself to the Creator and Sustainer of both East and West. With such an orientation, the community is confirmed in its bearings and it becomes finally possible to discern what constitutes measure and what proportion. In this, it can distinguish means and ends and relate the one to the other; it can balance freedom with morality as it seeks to retrieve and to relearn the essential wisdom that can preserve and ennoble the human species. In this way too it can 're-member' by putting its world back together and piecing the fragments into a whole.

Thus defined, the middle-most community is a community that is potentially inclusive of a humanity advancing at its own varying pace and temper to the center of an attracting magnetic field. It is a community that is selectively open to all who would freely elect to subscribe to its manifest and universally accessible principles, regardless of biological genes or of historical geographies and genealogies. In this sense, it is horizontally an expansive community by virtue of its membership and, vertically, an integrating of a radiating community by virtue of its principles. By definition, such a community would operate at a level which transcended the factitious East/West divide. The norms for a free and open encounter would be confirmed in the sense enjoined in the exhortation to consciously heed the meaning and consequences of our unitary origins.

> O mankind! We have created you out of a single pair of male and female, and We have made you into multiple nations and tribes, in order that ye may get to know one another. Truly, the most noble of you in the sight of God is the one who heeds God the most, who is most God-Conscious. (Qur'an 49:13)

And,

> O mankind! Be conscious of your Sustainer who has created you out of one living entity, and out of it created its mate, and out of the two spread forth a multitude of men and women. And remain conscious of God, in whose name you demand [your rights] from one another, and of these ties of kinship. Verily God is ever watchful over you. (Qur'an 4:1)

With the reconstituted perceptions of self and Other, and with a realistic attunement to the needs of an accelerating future, the agenda of the encounter could be set upon for action predicated on understanding. Having opted for retrieval and renewal, the retrieval of a common heritage and the renewal of an ailing humanity, the parties would then be expected to deliberate together on how a life-binding commitment could be optimally achieved – in time and with due measure.

NOTES

Prologue

1. S. Parvez Manzoor, "The Crisis of Muslim Thought and the Future of the Ummah" in Ziauddin Sardar, ed., *An Early Crescent: The Future of Knowledge and the Environment in Islam* (London: Mansell, 1989), pp.57-91. The excerpts which follow are taken from this article.

Chapter 1

1. The Institute is interested in soliciting the active collaboration of knowledgeable and dynamic elements who by virtue of training, background, experience, and proven interests could be expected to bring a genuine contribution to the realization of this project. Sponsoring round table discussions, assuming the format of brainstorming sessions to explore strategies of implementation, has been considered with this end in view. The idea is to steadily evolve a body of knowledgeable opinion on this field and to extend the debate to involve ever-widening circles of Muslim intellectual and cultural circles.

Chapter 2

1. *The Capitalist World Economy* (London: Cambridge University Press, 1979).
2. Cf. *The American Political Science Review* 82, no. 2 (June 1988), and *Journal of Politics* 50, no. 1 (February 1988) to which I have briefly alluded in an overview of trends in contemporary political thought. Mona Abul-Fadl, "Paradigms in Political Science Revisited: Muslim Perspectives" in *American Journal of Islamic Social Sciences, (AJISS)* 6, no. 1 (September 1989). Supplement. Also see "Contrasting Epistemics: The Vocationist, *Tawḥīd*, and Contemporary Social Theory," *American Journal of Islamic Social Sciences*, 7, no. 1 (March 1990).
3. In fact, F.S.C. Northrop, whose background was more with South East Asia in the post-War period, can be considered the father of the idea of an East/West cultural encounter when he first published *The Meeting of East and West: An Inquiry Concerning World Understanding* (New York: Macmillan, 1946). The theme could not have been too far from an ecumenically minded American opinion coming face

to face with its responsibilities as a newly emerging great power on the international scene. Cf. C.A. Robinson, *Alexander the Great: The Meeting of East and West in World Government* (Westport: Greenwood Press, 1984, c. 1947). The theme has been taken up in psychocultural and historical perspectives as the following titles suggest, *The Meeting of Two Worlds: Cultural Exchange between East and West during the Period of the Crusades* edited by Vladimir Goss and Christine Bornstien (Kalamazoo, MI: Medieval Institute Publications, Western Michigan University, 1986), and A.C. Paranjpe, *Theoretical Psychology: The Meeting of East and West* (New York: Plenum Press, 1984). Northrop's insights however, retain their originality and perhaps find some echoes in authors like C.P. Snow.

4. Renan became famous in the Muslim world for a historic debate he held with the great Muslim reformer of the age, Jamal al-Din al-Afghani (1838-1897). In fact, the apologetic discourse on the place of reason and rationality in modernist Muslim circles was provoked by the spirit of that encounter. Ironically, it took a Westernizing stance to place the "Renan phenomenon" in its proper context and to see the futility and the pathos of the Muslim reactions to it. See Edward Said, *Orientalism* (New York: Vintage, 1979), pp.130-48.
5. From the outset, the semantics of the term has been a problem both in English and in Arabic. Cf. *From Muslim to Islamic: The Proceedings of the Fourth Annual Convention of the AMSS* (Indianapolis: AMSS, 1975). Clearly the issue goes beyond semantics to substance, where the point is the principles underlying the pursuit of knowledge and the redefinition of a viable contemporary rationality shaped in the *tawḥīdī* perspective. Formulating this pursuit in terms of a new perspective on *daʿwah* in the modern setting has been perceptively remarked by Ziauddin Sardar in a compact overview on "Knowledge, Science and Islamization: A State of the Art Report" presented at the conference on the Future of the Ummah at Kuala Lumpur, 19-21 July 1987.
6. *The Venture of Islam, Conscience and History in World Civilization* (Chicago & London: University of Chicago Press, 1974). *The Classical World*, vol. 1. On the other hand, it could be argued that ideas retain a distinctiveness which reflects on the dynamic of their growth and spread. Unlike the production of commodities and the exercise of power where the traffic tends to be more concerted and patterns more authoritarian, this is not necessarily the case with the diffusion of culture. This underlies the remarks about the prospects of culture made above in chapter I.
7. Cf. Qur'an, 61:10 and 35:29. As a familiar idiom from the marketplace acquires moral and spiritual dimensions in Qur'anic usage, so too its extension to the social and cross-cultural domain exalts the notion of mutual interests and benefits beyond the confines of egoistic material concerns.

Chapter 3

1. See example in chapter 6.

2. The emphasis and priorities then were somewhat different as it was predominantly conceived in terms of educational/curriculum reform. See chapter 4.
3. The following excerpts are taken from the Prelude of the *Progress and Policy Report on the Western Thought Project* (PPR/WPT), Herndon, Va., December 1988.
4. Merryl Wyn Davies, *Knowing One Another: Shaping an Islamic Anthropology* (London: Mansell, 1988).
5. Ibid., p.53.

Chapter 4

1. See figure 3.
2. The late Ismaʿil Raji al-Faruqi (1339-1406/1921-1986) was born in Jerusalem and belonged to the first generation of a Palestinian diaspora that came to the United States in the early fifties. He graduated from the American University in Beirut in 1947 and returned briefly to an administrative post and later became the governor of the Upper Galilea in 1367/1948. He pursued his graduate studies in Indiana, Harvard and post doctorate studies at Al-Azhar and McGill and subsequently played an important role in promoting and developing Islamic study programs at American universities. He chaired the Department of Islamic Studies in Temple University which conducted one of the successful programs he had founded. In the sixties he played a key role in designing a curriculum in Islamics for the Islamic Research Institute in Islamabad, Pakistan, and by the latter seventies he was involved in several similar constructive ventures among Muslim communities throughout the globe. While a dedicated worker for a good cause, his energies were directed to the cultural and educational forum. Although he kept a low political profile, al-Faruqi never forgot his homeland and the predicament of his people (see his work *Islam and the Problem of Israel* [London: The Islamic Council of Europe, 1980]). His dynamic and productive life came to an abrupt end with the brutal assassination of himself and his life-long mate and dearest companion, Lois Lamya' al-Faruqi on 19th Ramadan 1405/27th May 1986. This is why he is referred to among those who have known him, worked with him and benefited from his dedication and his scholarship, as *al-Shahīd* – an honorific title of martyrdom given to Muslims who have spent their lives in a noble cause.
3. AbuSulayman is currently the President of the IIIT. He was formerly the Rector of the International Islamic University of Malaysia. Born in Makkah (1355/1936), educated in Cairo, Egypt, and the United States, he taught for some time at the University of King Saud in Riyadh where he played a key role in promoting grass-roots youth and cultural Islamic institutions on a national and international scale. He presided over the founding of the World Assembly of Muslim Youth in the seventies. Before going to Malaysia, he was the Director General at the International Institute of Islamic Thought and President of the Association of Muslim Social

Scientists. His doctoral dissertation, "The Islamic Theory of International Relations" (University of Pennsylvania (1394/1974), subsequently revised and published as a book, introduced new perspectives in Islamic methodology and political thought – a field to which he continues to make significant contributions.

4. The academic status and learning, the mobility, dynamism, and sheer exuberance of the late professor were all factors which assured him a prominent role in articulating and venting the ideas of this group in the circles of the English-speaking world. His intimate association with the group had led to a deepening of his own Islamic intellectual commitment in later years. That was the period which also saw his own major and original contributions to a vocational scholarship in works like *Trialogue of the Abrahamic Faiths, Toward Islamic English, Tawḥīd: Its Implications for Thought and Life, The Cultural Atlas of Islam* (a magnum opus which was co-authored with his wife, an original and creative scholar herself, and posthumously published by Macmillan).
5. A compact statement to this effect is found in a translated, edited, and notated version by Khurram Murad of a lecture delivered by Sayyid Abul A'la Mawdudi more than four decades ago, *Witnesses Unto Mankind* (The Islamic Foundation, Leicester, 1986).
6. This was the title of a conceptual framework pioneered at the Faculty of Economics and Political Science in the academic years 1981-1984 in a graduate course on Arab politics. Since then, aspects of this approach have been developed in dissertations and other work outside the academy.
7. This is another expression which has gained currency in contemporary Islamic thought in the Arabic-speaking world, and was first popularized in Sayyid Qutb's intensive writings on the subject, including his original and popular *tafsīr* (exegesis): *Fī Ẓilāl al-Qur'ān* [In the shade of the Qur'an].
8. Bernard McGrane, *Beyond Anthropology* (New York: Columbia University Press, 1989), one of the studies inspired by Michel Foucault's work in this field which is relevant to our own interests in a cultural hermeneutic, excavates the origins and evolution of the perception of self and other in the field of sociocultural anthropology in a manner that places the evolution of a discipline in its true historical and political perspectives.
9. Introducing this concept see articles on "Islamization as a Force of Global Cultural Renewal: or The Relevance of a *Tawḥīdī* Episteme to Modernity" in *AJISS*, 5, no.2 (December 1988) and "Contrasting Epistemics: *Tawḥīd*, the Vocationist and Social Science," *AJISS*, 7, no.1 (March 1990).

Chapter 5

1. See "The Art, the Artefact and the Artist: Introducing a Cultural Discourse." Also

see "Beyond Cultural Parodies and Parodizing Cultures: Shaping a Discourse" in the *American Journal of Islamic Social Sciences*, 8, No.1 (March 1991), pp.15-43.

2. See the *General Context Paper* above, chapter 2.

Chapter 6

1. This is the text of the preliminary *Working Paper* which was prepared for a round table held at the Institute in the Summer of 1409/1989. Its targeted audience was primarily, though not exclusively, Muslim, and its aim was to clarify aspects of the Western Thought Project and to impress the need to reconsider attitudes to the West from an independent and objective perspective as a test and condition for their own intellectual essor as Muslims. This sets the tone of the paper. I would also like to acknowledge the exchanges I had with Dr. Taha Jabir Alalwani on the subject while I was working on the draft for their influence in shaping and systematizing the ideas it presents.
2. It is important to distinguish between two levels in planning this project: the pedagogic level focusing on mastering the modern disciplines and producing authoritative textbooks to meet the educational needs of Muslim institutions. This is the level at which the Project is addressed in the official Prospectus of the Institute first published in 1402/1982, *Islamization of Knowledge: General Principles and Workplan.* The other level focuses on the broader intellectual and cultural dimensions of the Western heritage and assumes the educational goal within this broader perspective. This was the focus of *PPR/WTP.* The round table was invited to discuss the project in its broader perspective.
3. A more succinct statement on the objectives of the Project is found in the Introduction to *PPR/WTP.* The Report was drafted in a perspective that put the strategies of implementation in the context of the stated objectives. See above, chapter 3.
4. *Knowing One Another,* op. cit., p.132. Cf.115. In this chapter, the conceptual framework for an Islamic anthropology is developed by the author dextrously to produce the matrix for a viable inquiry grounded in the premises of the *tawḥīdī* paradigm of knowledge. In this latter context however such an anthropology is only the beginning for reconstructing a more holistic and unitary discipline for a restructured academia. Cf. p.174.
5. Ibid., p.140.
6. Cf. Davies. ibid., pp. 144-150. Our own proposal for joining in the dominant discourse in its own terms is only suggested as one possibility for communicating across paradigms; it is no substitute for the real task of constructing a self-sustaining matrix of discourse from within the *tawḥīdī* semantic field which is the only logical position consistent with the objectives of "Islamization." Accessing the dominant idiom is

part of the challenge of its reshaping and for going beyond it. Subscribing to existing rules can be no more than a temporary expedient to facilitate the encounter.

7. This consciousness exacts its moral consequences in a code of transactions based on *ʿadl, iḥsān, ṣidq, maʿrūf, taʿāruf, mawaddah, birr, taʿāwun* among others – some of which values are included in the above-mentioned sample of verses in the Qur'an. The conceptual/semantic field in the Qur'an is one of the rich virgin fields and has been broached in Muslim and non-Muslim scholarship. See Z. Sardar, *The Future of Muslim Civilization* (London: Croom and Helm, 1981) and an earlier attempt by T. Izutsu, *Ethico-Religious Concepts in the Qur'an* (Montreal: McGill Univ. Press, 1966). A relevant and concise inquiry related to this field is F. Denny's, "Ethics and the Qur'an: Community and Worldview," in *Ethics in Islam*, edited by R. G. Hovannisian (Malibu, Calif: Undena Publications, 1985), pp.103-21. In a renovationist Arabo-Islamic academy this is a burgeoning field. The case and method for approaching the Qur'an to reconstruct the matrix of a disciplinary inquiry is made in my *Naḥwa Minhājiyyah li al-Taʿāmul maʿa Maṣādir al-Tanẓīr al-Islāmī fī al-ʿUlūm al-Siyāsiyyah* paper presented at the Fourth International Conference of the Islamization of Knowledge held in Khartoum, January 1987. More specifically, the subject of a conceptual concordance of the Qur'an and Sunnah constitutes one of the priority programs in the Islamization of knowledge prospectus.

8. Charting cultural attitudes in the Muslim Ummah today has been briefly addressed above. See chapter 2.

9. *The Cultural Barrier: Problems in the Exchange of Ideas* (Edinburgh University Press, 1975). As the title suggests, the author's approach to cultural exchange is to examine those factors which inhibit communication in a practical context. "Within our own culture there is no 'alternative culture,' only some development or reshaping of what we inherit, and what is commonly meant by an alternative culture is more what we may call an 'anti-culture,' that is, the same culture expressed in reactive terms. When we come to communicate with people of different traditions it is essential that we should not deal with them exclusively ... in our own cultural terms . . ." This observation by the author sets the note for an enlightened and enlightening reading coming from within the Western tradition.

10. *The Great Ideas: A Syntopican of Great Books of the Western World* (Encyclopaedia Britannica, Inc., University of Chicago, Chicago [1952] 1990) 2 volumes. This was conceived as a basic reference work in the sphere of ideas and was intended to take its place in a triad which included dictionaries and encyclopaedias. The aim of the syntopical reading of the 517 works it covered was to locate the unity and continuity of Western thought in the discussion of common themes and problems from one end of the tradition to the other. It is not a digest of ideas as much as it is an index and a guide to the works themselves. My own approach to scanning and selecting such sources is described in part I of the *Progress Report* (**PPR/WTP**) referred to above.

11. This concept is developed in the context of European intellectual history by Hans Blumenberg in his epic writing on the subject. Cf. *The Legitimacy of the Modern Age*, trans. by Robert M. Wallace (Cambridge, MA: MIT, 1983), pp.455 ff. It could be used here to advantage in a critical reevaluation/periodization in Muslim cultural history. However, some earlier works of a comparable scale retain their value. See Karl Lowith, *The Meaning of History* (Chicago: University of Chicago, Phoenix, 1949).

Epilogue

1. Figures like the French philosopher and ethnologist, Ernest Renan, whose views are cited as an epigram in the opening of this collection. The quotation is taken from Vincent Monteil, *La Pensée Arabe* (Paris: Seghers, 1987). Like other orientalists, Renan left his marks on a generation of alienated Muslim thinkers, particularly in North Africa, who have sought to overcome their experiences of uprootedness and resolve their own ambivalences through intellectual and literary expression of varying caliber and "authenticity." For the European mindset at that epoch see Rana Kabbani, *Europe's Myths of Orient* (Bloomington: Indiana University Press, 1986).
2. *The World and I: A Chronicle of our Changing Era* 5, no.3 (March 1990): pp. 390-427 provides a representative sample of Havel's perceptive writing from his book *The Power of the Powerless* followed by an instructive commentary on his life and ideas.
3. This relates to an obscenity case brought before the Supreme Court in early 1990 by local authorities in Cincinnati, Ohio, led by the Citizens for Community Values. It was occasioned by the exhibition at the Contemporary Arts Center of controversial photographs of a deceased artist showing nudes and sadomasochistic and homoerotic activities which offended public sensibilities in one of the more propriety conscious midwestern cities in the United States. Robert Mapplethorpe (1946-1989) – who died of AIDS – used his art as a medium to promote the political agenda of homosexuals. For an informative overview of his artistic style and message see Eric Gibson in *The World and I* (November 1989), pp.211-15.
4. For a thorough and comprehensive overview and analysis placing the work in its relevant perspectives and highlighting its implications for a civilizational East/West encounter see Z. Sardar and M. W. Davies, *Distorted Imagination: Lessons from the Rushdie Affair* (London and Kuala Lumpur: Grey Seal and Berita, 1990).
5. See the "Fukuyama Debate" in *The National Interest* (Summer 1989 and Winter 1989-1990).
6. See above, chapter 3.
7. For relevant verses in this sense in the Qur'an see respectively, 6:164; 17:15; 53:38 and 2:286; 6:152; 23:62 and 2:134, 141.

8. Cf. The hadith of the Prophet, upon whom be peace, holds that 'every Muslim is outposted on a vigil to the Day of the Judgment.' See above, chapter 3. For the ethic of community and its implications for the Muslim historical consciousness see M. M. Abul-Fadl, *Alternative Perspectives: Islam from Within* (Leicester: The Islamic Foundation, 1990), chapter 4.

GENERAL INDEX